MERGERS AND ACQUISITIONS IN INDIA: A POST LIBERALISATION PERSPECTIVE

DR. JANKI MISTRY; DR. JAYDIP CHAUDHARI

Copyright © Dr. Janki Mistry; Dr. Jaydip Chaudhari
All Rights Reserved.

The book is dedicated to our students who keep alive our penchant for learning,
unlearning and relearning...

Contents

Preface

India remained a closed economy for way too long. By 1991, the country was on the verge of default. It was then that the economy was opened up wherein foreign players were allowed to open shop in India in a phased manner. The real growth of the country thus began in 1991 when the Indian economy embraced the open market system of Liberalisation, Privatisation and Globalisation in the year 1991. There has been no stopping the growth of the country, since then. The Gross Domestic Product of India has seen a steady increase over a period of time. Other economic indicators also have shown a positive trend. India ranks amongst the first three nations in terms of Foreign Direct Investments. The overall investment climate of the country has been positive in the last one and a half decade.

In this light, large scale Mergers and Acquisition activity has been recorded in India since the year 2000. The year 2007 was record breaker year for Mergers and Acquisitions in India, when deals worth around US $ 69.4 billion were struck. After, the global recession in the year 2008, M&A activity has once again gained pace. The year 2010 witnessed M&A activity of US $ 67.2 billion in India. India was ranked as the twelfth most favoured nation for M&As in the year 2010. Inbound as well as outbound deals have increased manifold in the recent years. Indian companies are on the global shopping spree! Many Indian companies have acquired giant conglomerates the world over.

Mergers and Acquisitions are strategies through which companies can grow and expand. Increasing size, gaining through economies of scale, entering new markets, acquiring new technology, increasing research and development strength, increasing product line etc. are a few reasons why companies resort to M&As.

Indian companies are riding on the high waves of a rapid economic growth, which further increases the need for speedy expansion. This need for fast growth has been further fueling the M&A activity in India.

There are several theories behind M&As which have been globally accepted. The most important one is the theory that M&As increase the efficiency of the firms under consideration. M&As are considered to be positive activities which can lead to growth, synergy and market power. M&A activities are taken up with the assumption that share holders' wealth will be enhanced. However, it has been noticed in many instances that

M&As do not create any positive value for the shareholders or the companies under consideration. There are many studies which prove that M&As do not create any value for the acquiring companies and sometimes they negatively impact the performance of the firms.

The book has been written to chart the merger and acquisition movement in India immediately after liberalisation. It comprehensively covers the Indian corporate landscape right from liberalisation to position where Indian companies started acquiring the world giants. It was the time of metamorphosis of the Indian industry. The book has tried to bring out how Indian companies emerged strong after a period of destabilisation post the LPG. The book has tried to cover the growth phase of the Merger and Acquisition movement in India.

Acknowledgements

The accomplishment of any task requires the help, support, and encouragement of many people. We are highly indebted to some persons who have played a very vital role in helping us complete this book.

We would like to thank the Almighty for giving us the confidence and good sense to take up this ambitious project.

We are grateful to Veer Narmad South Gujarat University and the Department of Business and Industrial Management for facilitating the production of this book. We would like to acknowledge the support of Dr. Manish Sidhpuria, Head of the Department, for helping us take the book forward.

We would like to render a special thank you to all our colleagues at the Department of Business and Industrial Management, Veer Narmad South Gujarat University, Surat. We would like to make a special mention of our colleague Dr. Dhaval Maheta who repeatedly motivated us to write a book. My special thanks to all the support and administrative staff of the Department of Business and Industrial Management as well as the Veer Narmad South Gujarat University.

We would like to thank our respective families for giving us the space and support required for completing this book.

Lastly, we thank all those whom we have not quoted unknowingly, but have helped us directly or indirectly in the completion of this book.

Janki Mistry
Jaydip Chaudhari

CHAPTER ONE

Global Historical Perspective of Mergers and Acquisitions

Over the centuries, Mergers & Acquisitions have been employed as strategic tools for achieving, growth, competitive advantage and creating wealthever-changingders. In today's ever changing, dynamic globalised environment, the M&A activity across the world is increasing at a rapid pace by creating new challenges and providing new opportunities to the companies involved. M&As are being widely used for improving competitiveness of companies through gaining greater market share, broadening the portfolio to reduce business risk, entering new markets and geographies, capitalizing on economies of scale etc.The year 2007 was a year for mega merger deals wherein the global deal value crossed US $ 4.7 trillion. According to the Boston Consulting Group (BCG), globally, approximately 23,000 deals were closed during the year 2010 which marked an increase of 7.6 percent over deal volume in the year 2009, while the value percent M&A deals rose 22.9 per cent to US $ 2.4 trillion. Emerging markets' M&A activity rose 76.2 per cent from the year 2009 to US $ 806.3 billion and accounted for 33 per cent of the total value of deals. The deal value of Indian M&As reached US $ 67.2 billion in the year 2010, barely missing the record of US $ 69.4 billion activity of the year 2007. In the first half of the year 2011, the global value of M&A deals has already reached US $ 1.5 trillion and India's inbound M&A volume was second highest in the Asia-Pacific region which surged to US $23.4 billion with the United Kingdom emerging as the top acquirer into India. Dealogic's ranking table reveals that India climbed from 16th to 12th position in global M&A transactions in the year 2010. Indian companies are transforming into MNCs and are snapping up assets across the globe, changing their market position rapidly. A slew of deals, including JSW Steel's purchase of a majority stake in Ispat Industries,

Reckitt Benckiser's tak,eover of Paras Pharmaceuticals and Tata Chemicals' acquisition of UK's British Salt, were announced during the last month of the year 2010. Some other recent examples are Hindalco acquiring Canada's Novelis for US $ 6 billion, becoming the world's largeand st aluminium rbecameompany, Bharti Airtel becoming the fifth largest telecom company in the world after its US $10 billion Zain deal.

Hence, it can be said that the M&A climate is very positive for India and the world. Many factors such as easr of getting finance, cash rich corporates and attractive growth and proliferation opportunities are said to be the driving force behind Merger and Acquisition activity which is expected to continue in a similar trend in future.

Historical Perspective of Strategy and Mergers and Acquisitions

Since times immemorial, mankind has inhabited the planet earth and will do so till the, end of the world. In the past it has been theorized that the principle of the survival of the FITTEST holds true. Then what happened to the Dinosaurs? The researcher has another theory—and that is the survival of the strategist. Man survived so long, not because he was the fittest, but because he strategically and systematically devised ways and means by which he could thrive in the wild, amongst the animals. As homosapiens gradually evolved to civilized human beings, their means, mind, and strategies evolved too.

Twenty five hundred years ago, Sun Tzu in his work titled "The Art of War" explained that the strategist seeks the state of *shih* - having positioned his forces at a place of advantage over rivals. In that same era, the Greek historian Thucydides wrote that the events of the past "will at some time or other, and in much the same ways, be repeated in the future." For the next 24 centuries, he has been proven correct time and again. Biographers of Napoleon Bonaparte talk about his ability to size up a situation with a single *coup d'oeil*, meaning "a stroke of the eye" or "glance." Napoleon was so knowledgeable about his strategic situation—the landscape, the enemy, available technology, similar situations from the past—that he could quickly transition ever- changing circumstances. The few things which are of utmost importance here are Enemy, Landscape, similar situations from the past and Ever changing circumstances. In the olden times, the strategies were mainly employed for the purpose of war or annexure of kingdoms. As man started moving away from his barbaric ways and tried to establish order and harmony in his social life, war strategies took many new forms. This book deals with strategy from the management point of view. It would not be wrong to say that making a success out of your business is like winning a war. Revisiting Napolean - **Enemy** in war is like competition in business, **Landscape in war** is the Economic, political and social environment in Business, **Ever changing circumever-changing** are similar to ever changing climate of the market and economy in business. So, in the life or death quest for strategic change, business has much to learn from war. Both are about the same thing: succeeding in competition. Even more basic, both can be distilled to four words: informed choice/timely action. The key objective in competition - whether business or war - is to improve the organization's performance along these dimensions:

- To generate better information than rivals
- To analyze that information and make sound choices
- To make those choices quickly
- To convert strategic choices into decisive action

In simple words, strategy, from the point of view of business management is a decision or a series of decisions takethe n in order to be able to beat competition and adapt to some major change in the existing environment of business for the ultimate growth or sustainability of the enterprise.

Mergers, acquisitions and all the different types of corporate restructuring activities can be classified as strategies or quasi strategies adapted by businesses to achieve growth, expand, disseminate value and basically become better equipped to face competition.

Mergers and Acquisitions are nothing but strategic alliances between companies. These types of transactions can be referred to as alliances as they are usually beneficial to both – the acquiring party as well as the selling party.

Strategic alliances have very deep rooted history. One can start with the first emperor of India- Chandragupta Maurya (320 BCE-298 BCE). It is said that his kingdom ranged from Bengal and Assam in East India to Kashmir and Nepal in the North, the Deccan plateau and much of Southern India. It is believed that Alexander the Great came to India and conquered much of the Northern Province (now Afghanistan and Pakistan) and he fought with king Porus on the banks of the river Beas. Although he defeated king Porus, his troupes were heavily damaged and he had to return to Greece. However, he left the regions he had conquered in the care of his Satraps[1](A subordinate bureaucrat official). Chandragupta Maurya had already annexed most of Northern India with the help of his chief strategist Chanakya after which he started taking a stronghold in Alexander's Satrapies. Seleucus I Nicator, the then Satrap of Alexander, who was well aware of the prowess of the emperor, struck an alliance with Chandragupta Maurya. The alliance was such that Chandragupta Maurya married Seleucus's daughter and obviously got the Satrapies as dowry and in return he gave 500 war elephants to Seleucus!

The Rajputs of Marwar have been known for their strategy of conquest through forging matrimonial alliances. The glaring example is that of the marriage of princess Jodha, daughter of King Bharmal of Amer to King Akbar. Political success knew no bounds for Emperor Akbar. After having secured the Hindu Kush, his empire extended from Afghanistan to the Bay of Bengal, and from the Himalyas to the Narmada. However, the Rajputs of the Western regions of India were giving him a tough time. Through a shrewd blend of diplomacy, intimidation and brute force, Akbar won the allegiance of the Rajputs. He married Jodhaa, a fiery Rajput princess, in order to further strengthen his relations with the Rajputs. The alliance of Jodha and Akbar it was, but it was more of a political allegiance of the Rajput states to King Akbar, whereby the Rajput states, to an extent retained their autonomy, but in turn were a part of Akbar's Dynasty.

These are but, just a few of the innumerable such strategic political alliances which have taken place throughout history in different parts of the world.

Mergers and Acquisitions in businesses can be termed as derivatives of such historical alliances.

Business Mergers, Acquisitions and Takeovers first started in 1890s and the United States of America recorded the most important M&A activity during this period.

[1] From Latin *satrapa,* from Greek *satrapēs,* from Old Persian *khshathrapāvan,* Meaning: protector of the land. King Darius I of Persia employed the system of dividing their territory into *satrapies*, or provinces, over which a satrap was put in charge. Alexander liked the idea and kept the administrative structure.

The Rajputs of Marwar have been known for their strategy of conquest through forging matrimonial alliances. The glaring example is that of the marriage of princess Jodha, daughter of King Bharmal of Amer to King Akbar. Political success knew no bounds for Emperor Akbar. After having secured the Hindu Kush, his empire extended from Afghanistan to the Bay of Bengal, and from the Himalayas to the Narmada river. However, the Rajputs of the Western regions of India were giving him a tough time. Through a shrewd blend of diplomacy, intimidation, and brute force, Akbar won the allegiance of the Rajputs. He married Jodhaa, a fiery Rajput princess, in order to further strengthen his relations with the Rajputs. The alliance of Jodha and Akbar it was, but it was more of a political allegiance of the Rajput states to King Akbar, whereby the Rajput states, to an extent, retained their autonomy, but in turn, was a part of Akbar's Dynasty.

These are but, just a few of the innumerable such strategic political alliances which have taken place throughout history in different parts of the world.

Mergers and Acquisitions in businesses can be termed as derivatives of such historical alliances.

Business Mergers, Acquisitions, and Takeovers first started in the 1890s and the United States of America recorded the most important M&A activity during this period.

[1] From Latin *satrapa,* from Greek *satrapēs,* from Old Persian *khshathrapāvan,* Meaning: protector of the land. King Darius I of Persia employed the system of dividing their territory into *satrapies,* or provinces, over which a satrap was put in charge. Alexander liked the idea and kept the administrative structure.

CHAPTER TWO

Early Merger Movements in the USA

The Early Merger Movements of the USA:

Several countries have experienced high levels of M&A activity in the past. The USA has the longest history of substantial takeover activity going back to the 1890s. Several Merger movements have occurred in the United States and each was more or less dominated by a particular type of merger. All of the merger movements occurred when the economy experienced sustained high rates of growth and coincided with particular developments in business environments.

The different merger waves in the USA have been characterized as follows:

The FIRST wave (1895-1904):

This wave mainly consisted of horizontal mergers, which resulted in high concentration in many industries, including heavy manufacturing industries. The period was one of rapid economic expansion. In this wave the industrial production grew by 100 per cent. This wave involved an estimated 15 per cent of all manufacturing assets and employees. An important characteristic of this merger wave was the simultaneous consolidation of producers within industries, thus qualifying for the description 'horizontal consolidation.' Many of the giants of the US corporate world such as General Electric, Eastman Kodak, American Tobacco and DuPont were formed during the first wave through such consolidation. Approximately seventy one important oligopolistic or near competitive industries were converted into near monopolies by merger. More than 1800 firms disappeared into consolidations. Of the approximately 93 consolidations, 72 controlled as least 40 per cent market share and 42 controlled at least 70 per cent of their industries. Although the

Sherman Act[1]to control and prevent monopolies had come into effect in the year 1890, it had little immediate effect on the progress or the ferocity of the first wave. This movement peaked in the year 1899 and almost ended in the year 1903 when a severe economic depression set in. The year 1904 decision of the Supreme Court in the Northern Securities case[2] may have contributed to ending the merger wave.

The SECOND wave (1916-1929):

This wave was a much smaller one than the first wave in terms of its relative impact. In total it involved less than 10 per cent of the economy's assets. Many combinations in this period occurred outside the previously consolidated heavy manufacturing industries. The public utilities and banking industries were among the most active. About 60 per cent of the mergers occurred in the food processing, chemicals and mining sectors. A large portion of mergers in the 1920s represented product extension mergers as in the cases of IBM, General Foods and Allied Chemicals, market extension mergers in food retailing, department stores, motion picture theatres, and vertical mergers in the mining and metals industries. Since, the Sherman Act had proved to be ineffective, the Clayton Act[3]was passed which basically labeled monopolies as illegal. The second wave accompanied economic growth and stock market boom in the USA. The second wave gave rise to many oligopolistic industrial structures. It however, collapsed in the year 1929 with the stock market crash of that year and in the following four years of worldwide depression, many of the utility holding companies formed collapsed into bankruptcy.

The merger movement between 1940 and 1947:

The Second World War and the early post war years were accompanied by rapid growth of the economy and an upsurge in merger activity. Lacking any significant changes in technological and business environments, however, the merger movement was much smaller than the earlier ones.

The THIRD wave (1965-1969):

The mergers that took place during this period (1965-69) were mainly conglomerate mergers. Mergers were inspired by high stock prices, interest rates and strict enforcement of antitrust laws. The Bidder firms in the third wave merger were smaller than the Target Firms. Mergers were financed from equities; the investment banks no longer played an important role. The major industries which saw the merger movement during this phase were aerospace, industrial machinery, railway equipment, auto parts, textiles, and tobacco. These kinds of mergers were sponsored by equities, thereby eliminating the roles of banks which they actively played in investment activities earlier. In the year 1968, the Attorney General decided to break the multinationals which resulted in the end of merging activities after that. The decision was triggered by the inefficient performance of the multinationals. But the 1970s saw the emergence of mergers which made their mark by performing effectively. Some mergers in the 1970s which have set precedence were the INCO(International Nickel Company)-ESB merger; United Technologies and OTIS Elevator Merger and the merger between Colt Industries and Garlock Industries.

The FOURTH wave (1981-1989):

The late 1970s witnessed a small revival of takeover activity but this did not last long owing to the second oil crisis in the year 1979 and the deep recession of the early 1980s. It was in the middle of the 1980s that there was a fresh surge of takeover activity leading to the fourth merger wave in US history. This wave actually consisted of two waves-acquisitions and divestitures. These two types of corporate restructuring activities are highly correlated with a correlation coefficient of 0.95 (Sudarsanam, 2009). Divestitures generally constituted 20-40 percent of the M&A activity during this period. Thus many US corporations engaged in simultaneous expansion and downsizing of their businesses, expanding those that offered scope for greater competitive advantage and exiting those in which their historic competitive advantage had been eroded. Many US companies not only made numerous acquisitions but also sold off some of their component businesses in a move toward increasing the focus of their business portfolio and restricting it to what they deemed were core businesses in which they judged themselves to have a competitive advantage. The fourth wave subsided after the year 1989 and the fifth wave enveloped the US economy from the year 1993 to the year 2000.

The FIFTH wave (1990-2000):

The fifth wave of the 1990s to some extent continued the theme of focus on core competencies as the source of competitive advantage. The fifth wave can be called the mother of all the previous waves as the deal sizes in terms of values and numbers assumed gigantic proportions. In the year 2000, the value of M&A deals was US$ 1.8 trillion as compared to the previous peak of US$ 324 billion in the year 1989. In this phase, the firms started making acquisitions on the basis of the need to augment their resources and capabilities in order to enhance their competitive advantage. The 1990s saw the emergence of new technologies such as the Internet, cable television, and satellite communication, which spawned new industries and firms with new technological capabilities. Starting in the fourth merger wave (1992–1998) and continuing today, companies are more likely to acquire in the same business, or close to it, firms that complement and strengthen an acquirer's capacity to serve customers. Buyers aren't necessarily hungry for the target companies' physical assets. Now they're going after entirely different prizes. The hot prizes aren't things—they're thoughts, methodologies, people, and relationships. Many companies are being bought for their patents, licenses, market share, name brand, research staff, methods, customer base, or culture. Soft capital, like this, is very perishable, fragile, and fluid. Integrating it usually takes more finesse and expertise than integrating machinery, real estate, inventory, and other tangibles.

Hence, it may be said that the evolution of mergers and acquisitions has been long drawn. Many economic factors have contributed to its development. There are several other factors that have impeded their growth. As long as economic units of production exist mergers and acquisitions would continue for an ever-expanding economy.

The SIXTH wave (year 2003 onwards):
The last wave of Mergers and restructuring activities can be said to have started in the year 2003 and is still continuing. This wave is characterized by deals in which corporate governance and shareholder activism, are of primary importance. Deals have now reached such humongous proportions that LBOs have become the dominant method for acquisitions. Private equity deals are also on the increase.

[1] The Sherman Act was passed in 1890 and was named after its author, Senator John Sherman, an Ohio Republican, the chairman of the Senate Finance Committee, who was also Rockefeller's colleague. The purpose of the Act was to oppose the combination of entities that could potentially harm competition, such as monopolies or cartels and today still forms the basis for most antitrust litigation by the United States federal government.

[2]***Northern Securities Co. v. the United States***, 192 U.S. 197 (1904), was an important ruling by the U.S. Supreme Court. The Court ruled 5 to 4 against the stockholders of the Great Northern and Northern Pacific railroad companies, who had essentially formed a monopoly and to dissolve the Northern Securities Company. The company was sued in 1902 under the Sherman Antitrust Act of 1890 by President Theodore Roosevelt, one of the first anti-trust cases filed against corporate interests instead of labor

[3]*A federal law enacted in 1914 as an amendment to the* Sherman Anti-Trust Act. Substantively, the act seeks to capture anticompetitive practices in their incipiency by prohibiting particular types of conduct, not deemed in the best interest of a competitive market. There are 4 sections of the bill that proposed substantive changes in the antitrust laws by way of supplementing the Sherman Act of 1890. In those sections, the Act thoroughly discusses the following four principles of economic trade and business: price discrimination, which is the sale of the same product to comparably situated buyers at different prices; tying and exclusive dealing contracts, which are the sale of products on condition that the buyer stop dealing with the seller's competitors; corporate mergers, the acquisition of competing companies by one company; and interlocking directorates, the members of which are common members on the boards of directors of competing companies.

CHAPTER THREE

Merger Waves in the European Union

The EU member countries have experienced increasing levels of takeover activity since the year 1984. Two waves can be identified for this region; a small one during the years 1987-1992 and a vastly bigger one between the years 1995 and 2001. The late 1980s and the 1990s which accompanied the two merger waves in the EU have been epochal and turbulent times in the history of the continent. This was a period of continual changes with newer and ever more audacious initiatives being taken in the spheres of politics, economics and the social institutions to further European integration. Among them, are the Single Market initiative, which came into effect in the year 1992, and the European Economic and Monetary Union project[1], which has ushered in monetary union among 12 out of 15 member states with the introduction of a single currency euro from the year 1999. This was also the period when the Cold War[2] ended, the Berlin Wall collapsed and the countries of Eastern and Central Europe started dismantling state controls of their economies and adopting free markets and private enterprise with enthusiasm and passion.

These historic events were also accompanied by the spread of deregulation and privatization by member states to improve the competitiveness of the EU economies. Although stock markets have traditionally been less important as a source of funding for EU firms, apart from UK firms, than in the US, the stock markets experienced prolonged bull phases. The technological changes in information technology, telecommunications, biotechnology etc. provided new growth opportunities which the EU firms sought to exploit through mergers and acquisitions.

Merger Waves in the United Kingdom:

Active merger movement in the UK can be traced to the 1960s, although two mini merger booms happened in the 1890s and 1920s. The 1960s and 1980s merger waves in the US have a striking parallel to the merger waves in the US during the same period.

The first wave peaking in the year 1968 was largely fuelled by horizontal mergers. This characteristic differentiates the UK wave from the US wave of the same period. The latter represented a shift from monopolistic and oligopolistic mergers of the first two waves to conglomerate mergers. Under the Labour government of the year 1964, a new industrial policy was adopted to strengthen the UK companies into 'national champions' that could take on competitors on world markets. The Industrial Reorganization Corporation was the newly created instrument for bringing about this transformation. During the years 1965-69, Industrial Reorganisation Corporation sponsored approximately 50 horizontal mergers. The mergers sponsored by the IRC generally escaped antitrust scrutiny by the Monopolies and Mergers Commission.

The second wave that peaked in the year 1972 was also characterized by horizontal mergers but on a slightly smaller scale. There was also greater incidence of conglomerate mergers. While horizontal mergers accounted for 82 per cent of number and 89 per cent of assets involved in mergers considered by the Mergers Panel of the MMC during the years 1965-69, in the following wave, in the years 1970-74, the corresponding figures are 73 per cent and 65 per cent respectively.

The third wave was of tidal proportions as compared to the previous two. As in the US, this wave coincided with a stock market bull run from the recession of the years 1980-81 to the market crash in the year 1987. Massive restructuring was seen in the manufacturing industries and in the financial services sector in the 1980s. The BIG BANG DEREGULATION[3] of the financial services sector in the City of London heralded the arrival of the US investment banks, which brought not only their huge capital raising capabilities but also their investment banking expertise and techniques in the areas of mergers and acquisitions advisory work, corporate restructuring, risk management, securities trading and stockbroking. The effect of the Big Bang on the Financial sector in the UK can be termed as cataclysmic as most of the British merchant banks, brokerage houses and securities firms were systematically swallowed up, initially by American and subsequently by continental European companies.

The fourth wave happened in the 1990s when UK experienced a series of privatizations. Sectors such as water, electricity and gas were privatized. Further deregulation of the telecom industry took place, increasing pressure on British Telecom- a monopoly-to restructure. Many firms undertook divestitures.

Global Scenario of Mergers and Acquisitions:

The Global M&A Scenario from the years 1992 to 2006 has been shown in Chart 1.1. The year 2000 was a very prominent year for mergers and acquisitions globally. Deals worth around 4000 billion Euros (Approximately US $ 5785.68 billion) were struck in the year 2000. The year 2006 followed suit with around 3700 billion Euros (US $ 5351 billion).

Chart No. 1 - Historical Perspective of the Global M&A Scenario (1992-2006)

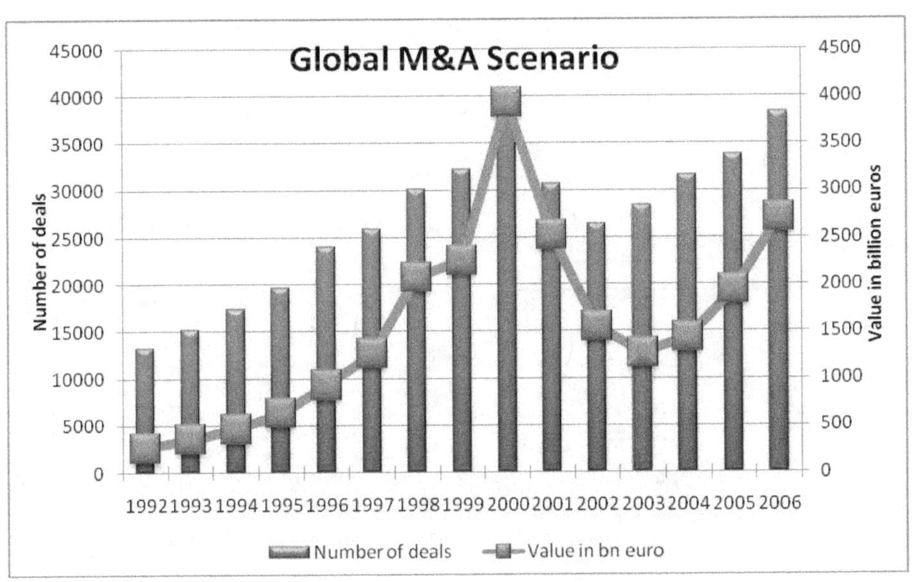

(Source: www.worksproject.be/documents/Buelens.ppt)

The following tables show some of the biggest M&A deals globally between the years 1990 to 1999 and the years 2000 to 2010. The Vodafone Airtouch PLC and Mannesman Merger was the largest in the year 1999 which amounted to US $ 183,000 millions. Total value of top 10 deals amounted to US $ 742,560 millions.

Table No. 1 – Top 10 Global Mergers & Acquisitions (1990-1999)

Rank	Year	Purchaser	Target	Transaction value (US $ Millions)
1	1999	Vodafone Airtouch PLC	Mannesmann	183,000
2	1999	Pfizer	Warner-Lambert	90,000
3	1998	Exxon	Mobil	77,200
4	1998	Citicorp	Travelers Group	73,000
5	1999	SBC Communications	Ameritech Corporation	63,000
6	1999	Vodafone Group	AirTouch Communications	60,000
7	1998	Bell Atlantic	GTE	53,360
8	1998	BP	Amoco	53,000
9	1999	Qwest Communications	US WEST	48,000
10	1997	Worldcom	MCI Communications	42,000

(Source: http://en.wikipedia.org/wiki/
Mergers_and_acquisitions#Major_M.26A)

Table No. 2 – Top 10 Global Mergers & Acquisitions (2000-2010)

Rank	Year	Purchaser	Target	Transaction value (US $ Millions)
1	2000	*Fusion*: America Online Inc. (AOL)	Time Warner	164,747
2	2000	Glaxo Wellcome Plc.	SmithKline Beecham Plc.	75,961
3	2004	Royal Dutch Petroleum Co.	Shell Transport & Trading Co	74,559
4	2006	AT&T Inc.	BellSouth Corporation	72,671
5	2001	Comcast Corporation	AT&T Broadband & Internet Svcs	72,041
6	2009	Pfizer Inc.	Wyeth	68,000
7	2000	*Spin-off*: Nortel Networks Corporation		59,974
8	2002	Pfizer Inc.	Pharmacia Corporation	59,515
9	2004	JP Morgan Chase & Co	Bank One Corp	58,761
10	2008	Inbev Inc.	Anheuser-Busch Companies, Inc	52,000

(Source: http://en.wikipedia.org/wiki/
Mergers_and_acquisitions#Major_M.26A)

Table No. 3 - Top Mergers and Acquisitions deals worldwide by value ($20 billion or larger) from 2010 to 2020

Rank	Year	Purchaser	Purchased	Transaction value	Inflation adjusted
46	2010	GDF Suez	International Power	30	37.3
52	2011	Express Scripts	Medco Health Solutions	29.1	35.1
45	2012	Glencore	Xstrata	31	36.6
1	2013	Verizon Communications	Vodafone Group (Verizon Wireless 45% Stake)	130	151.2
13	2014	Kinder Morgan	Kinder Morgan Energy Partners	71	81.3
2	2015	Dow Chemical	E. I. du Pont de Nemours and Company	130	148.6
8	2016	AT&T	Time Warner	85.4	96.4
7	2017	Linde AG	Praxair	86	95.1
6	2018	Energy Transfer Equity	Energy Transfer Partners	90	97.1
3	2019	United Technologies (Aerospace Division)	Raytheon	121	128.2
2	2020	Unilever plc	Unilever N.V.	81	84.8

Source:- https://en.wikipedia.org/wiki/
Mergers_and_acquisitions#Major_M.26AEnter Caption

Chart No. 2 - Inflation adjsuted trnsaction value of the top deals between 2010 to 2020

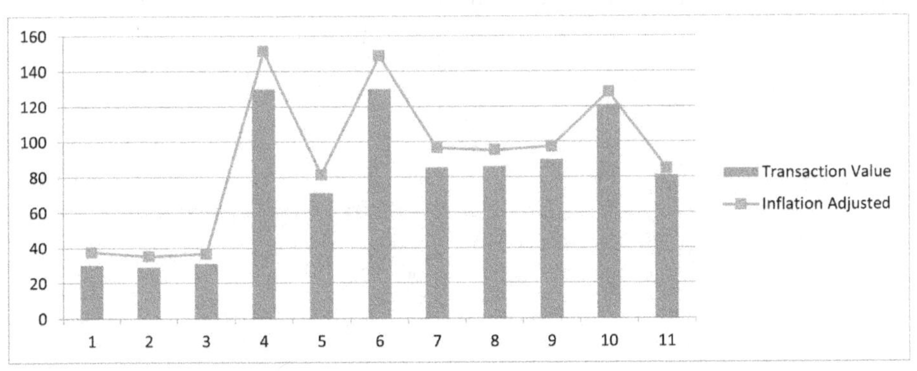

Source:- https://en.wikipedia.org/wiki/
Mergers_and_acquisitions#Major_M.26A

The total transaction value was maximum in the years 2013 and 2015 followed by the year 2019.

[1] The **Economic and Monetary Union (EMU)**is an umbrella term for the group of policies aimed at converging the economies of members of the European Union in three stages so as to allow them to adopt a single currency, the euro. As such, it is largely synonymous with the Eurozone.

[2]Cold War was the conflict between the Communist nations led by the erstwhile Soviet Union and the democratic nations led by the United States. It was fought by all means - propaganda, economic war, diplomatic haggling and occasional military clashes. There were deep-rooted ideological, economic and political differences between the United States and the Soviet Union before the Second World War. These differences were intensified as a result of their mutual suspicions immediately after the Second World War which led to a situation of cold war between them.

[3] The phrase **Big Bang**, used in reference to the sudden deregulation of financial markets, was coined to describe measures, including abolition of fixed commission charges and of the distinction between stockjobbers and stockbrokers on the London Stock Exchange and change from open-outcry to electronic, screen based trading, enacted by the United Kingdom government in 1986. In the UK, Big Bang became one of the cornerstones of the Thatcher government's reform programme. Prior to these reforms, the once-dominant financial institutions of the city of London were failing to compete with foreign banking. The effects of Big Bang were dramatic, with London's place as a financial capital decisively strengthened, to the point where it arguably became the world's most important financial centre.

CHAPTER FOUR

The History of M&As in India

M&As have played an important role in the transformation of the industrial sector of India since the Second World War period. The economic and political conditions during the Second World War and post–war periods gave rise to a spate of M&As. The inflationary situation during the wartime enabled many Indian businessmen to amass income by way of high profits, dividends and black money. This led to "wholesale infiltration of businessmen in industry during war period giving rise to hectic activity in stock exchanges. There was a craze to acquire control over industrial units in spite of swollen prices of shares. The practice of cornering shares in the open market and trafficking of managing agency rights with a view to acquiring control over the management of established and reputed companies had come prominently to light. The net effect of these two practices, i.e. of acquiring control over ownership of companies and of acquiring control over managing agencies, was that large number of concerns passed into the hands of prominent industrial houses of the country. As it became clear that India would be gaining independence, British managing agency houses gradually liquidated their holdings at fabulous prices offered by the Indian Business community. Besides, the transfer of managing agencies, there were a large number of cases of transfer of interests in individual industrial units from British to Indian hands. Further at that time, it used to be the fashion to obtain control of insurance companies for the purpose of utilizing their funds to acquire substantial holdings in other companies. The big industrialists also floated banks and investment companies for furtherance of the objective of acquiring control over established concerns. The post-war period is regarded as an era of M&As. Large number of M&As occurred in industries like jute, cotton textiles, sugar, insurance, banking, electricity and tea plantation. It has been found that, although there were a large number of M&As in the early post independence period[1], the anti-big government policies and regulations of the 1960s and 1970s seriously deterred M&As. This does not mean that M&As were uncommon during the controlled regime. The deterrent was mostly to horizontal combinations which result in concentration of economic power to the common detriment. However, there were many conglomerate combinations. In some cases, even the Government encouraged M&As; especially for sick units.

Certain historic Mergers/amalgamations did take place which are worthy of mention.

Bank of Hindustan, set up in the year 1870, was the earliest Indian Bank. Banking in India on modern lines started with the establishment of three presidency banks under Presidency Bank's act of the year 1876 i.e. Bank of Calcutta, Bank of Bombay and Bank of Madras. In the year 1921, all presidency banks were amalgamated to form the Imperial Bank of India.

Life Insurance Corporation(LIC) of India was incorporated in the year 1956 with the amalgamation of over 200 insurance companies and provident societies. Previously, it was known as Oriental Life Insurance Company. The company was the first to offer life coverage in India. There was a similar development in the general insurance business.

The National Textiles Corporation (NTC) took over a large number of sick textiles units.

In the year 1950, the Goenka Group acquired two British trading houses namely the Duncan Brothers and Octavius Steel. They also had some successful acquisitions in the areas of tea, automobiles, tyres, jute, electric cables and cotton textiles.

The functional importance of M&As is undergoing a sea change since liberalisation in India. The MRTP Act and other legislations have been amended paving way for large business groups and foreign companies to resort to the M&A route for growth. Further The SEBI (Substantial Acquisition of Shares and Take over) Regulations, of the years 1994 and 1997, have been notified. The decision of the Government to allow companies to buy back their shares through the promulgation of buy back ordinance, and other such developments, have influenced the market for corporate control in India. M&As, as strategies were employed by several corporate groups like R.P. Goenka, Vijay Mallya and Manu Chhabria for growth and expansion of their empires in India in the eighties. Some of the companies taken over by RPG group included Dunlop, Ceat, Philips Carbon Black and Gramaphone India. The first of the acquisitions was CEAT Tyres of India in the year 1981. The group then went on to acquire KEC (1982); Searle India, now RPG Life Sciences (1983); Dunlop (1984); Gramophone Company of India Ltd, now Saregama India (1986); and finally CESC, Harrisons Malayalam, Spencer & Co. and ICIL, all in 1989.

Vijay Mallya's United Breweries (UB) group was straddled mostly by M&As. Further, in the post liberalization period, the giant Hindustan Lever Limited has employed M&A as an important growth strategy. The Ajay Piramal group has almost entirely been built up by M&As. The south based, Murugappa group built an empire by employing M&A as a strategy. Some of the companies acquired by Murugappa group includes, EID Parry, Coromondol Fertilizers, Bharat Pulverising Mills, Sterling Abrasives, Cut Fast Abrasives etc. Other companies and groups whose growth has been contributed by M&As include Ranbaxy Laboratories Limited and Sun Pharmaceuticals Industries particularly during the latter half of the 1990s. During this decade, there had been a plethora of M&As happening in every sector of Indian economy. Even, the known and big industrial houses of India, like Reliance Group, Tata Group and Birla group have engaged in several big deals.

[1] Post independence, for about 10 years India was receptive towards foreign investment due to various reasons. Thereafter due to change in policies, India became a closed economy. Hence it became nearly impossible for an Indian business firm to think of inviting foreign investment, leave alone investing abroad. The concept of M&As gained popularity in India, after the government introduced the new economic policy in 1991, thereby paving the way for economic reforms and opening up a whole lot of challenges both in the domestic and international spheres.

Table No. 4 – Total Number of M&As in India between 1990 and 2000

Year	Non-Manufacturing	Manufacturing	Total
1990-1995	116	175	291
1995-2000	233	510	743
2001-2010	349	685	1034

(Source: www.igidr.ac.in/money)

Table No. 5 - Total number of M&A in India between 2011-2020

YEAR	NON - MANUFACTURING	MANUFACURING	TOTAL
2011-2020	897	473	1370

(Source: www.igidr.ac.in/money)

It can be seen from table no. 5 that the total number of deals in the non-manufacturing sector had increased to 897 from 349 in the previous decade. The total number of deals in the manufacturing sector were 473. A total of 1370 deals occured from 2011 to 2020.

Table No. 6 - Distribution of M&A across Industry Groups from 1990-91 to 2000-01

Industry/Year	1990 - 91	1991 - 92	1992 - 93	1993 - 94	1994 - 95	1995 - 96	1996 - 97	1997 - 98	1998 - 99	1999 - 00	2000 - 01	Total
Pharmaceuticals				2	0	5	27	47	29	57	34	201
Petrochemicals.						4	11	5	11	13	13	57
Energy, Gas, Power				1	0	3	6	13	15	16	17	71
Non metallic minerals					2	3	2	11	11	19	7	55
Food products			3	1	2	8	8	10	9	20	13	74
Textiles, weaving	1	0	0	0	1	0	4	4	12	6	6	34
IT & telecom				3	0	0	11	20	31	45	51	161
Electricals, electronics				2	0	0	7	11	13	11	13	57
Basic metals, alloys				1	3	4	9	13	15	15	11	71
Equipment, machinery				4	3	2	12	26	25	30	11	113
Transport equipment						1	4	13	13	24	10	65
Tobacco, beverages				2	2	0	0	4	3	5	6	22
Others							12	31	37	61	58	199
TOTAL M & A	1	0	4	16	14	33	124	248	269	387	290	1386

(Source: www.igidr.ac.in/money)

In the decade, 1990 to 2001, the maximum number of deals took place in teh pharmaceutical sector followed by 161 deals in textiles and weaving sector . 113 deals took place in the equipment and machinery sector and 71 deals took place in the energcy, gas and power sector.

The maximum number of deals took place in the year 1999-2000 followed by 290 deals in 2000-01. The increase in the number of deals since 1997-98 had been on an increasing trend.

Table No. 7 - Distribution of M&A Across Industry Groups from 2011-2020

Industry/Year	2011-12	2012-13	2013-14	2014-15	2015-16	2016-17	2017-18	2018-19	Total
Pharma				40	35		34	39	148
Petrochemicals	1	4	0	0	0	5	10	12	32
Non Metallics	2	2	3	0	0	20	29	32	88
Food Product	25	2	15			5	16	10	73
Textile	1	0				4	12	6	23
IT & Telecom	0	0	0	0	19	15	20	55	109
Machinery	0	13	19			35	45	55	135
Transport	1			4	5	10	24	11	55
Tobacco	12	11		3	6	16			48
Other						12	37	58	107
TOTAL M&A	**42**	**32**	**37**	**47**	**65**	**110**	**190**	**278**	**818**

(Source: www.igidr.ac.in/money)

Chart No. 3 - Distribution of M&A across sectors (1990-91 to 2000-01)

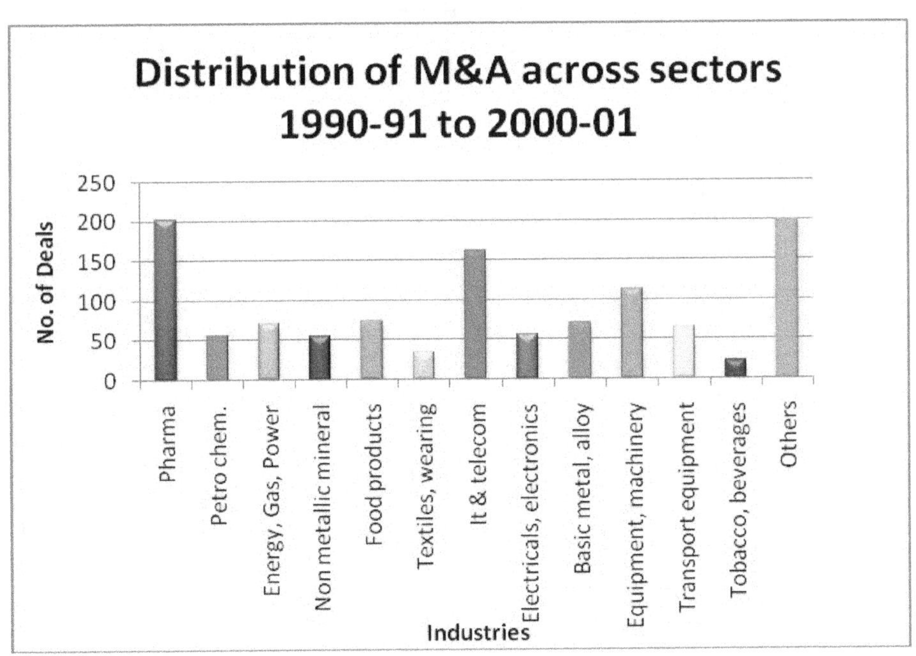

(Source: www.igidr.ac.in/money)

Chart No. 4 - Distribution of M&A across sectors (2010-2020)

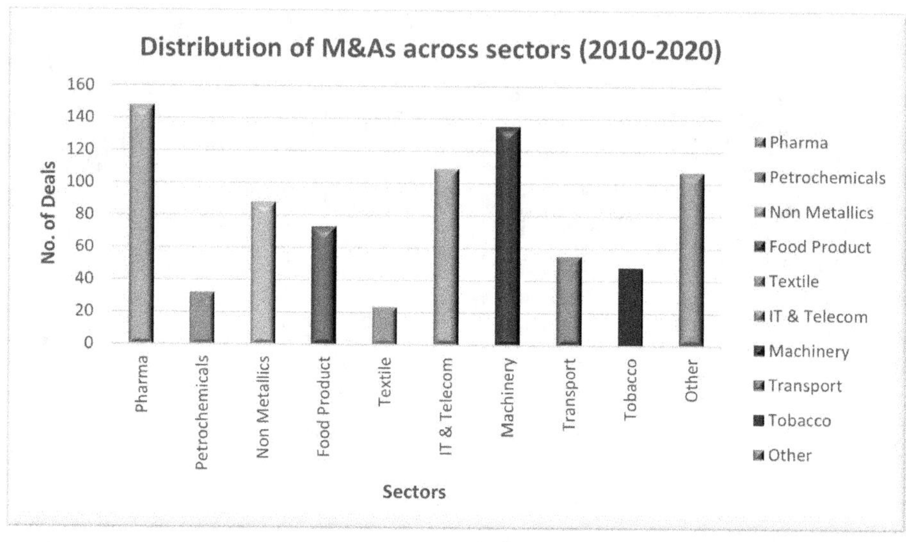

(Source: www.igidr.ac.in/money)

CHAPTER FIVE

The Change in Economic Climate in India and the emergence of systematic M&A Activity

India forayed into the Liberalisation era after the year 1991. In the erstwhile economic structure before the nineties, in the times of licensing and quota system, expansion was a crime. But after the opening up of the economy in the early nineties by the government, when Indian monopolies were challenged by global business houses, the real meaning of competition dawned upon the industries. World class quality, a plethora of products and services available from foreign competitors, latest technology used by foreign players etc. lead to a situation where survival of the fittest started becoming a norm. It was not easy for Indian companies to plunge into the LPG era as there were several challenges that Indian business houses had to face with the opening up of the economy. There was wide scale change in the business and political environment of the country. Listed below are some of the challenges faced by Indian companies post liberalization:

The Business Challenges of a Liberalised Economy and the need for growth:

The destabilization due to Entrepreneurial freedom:

- The cocoon of protection enjoyed so far by existing players disappeared. Everyone now had to compete in an open and competitive market. Monopolistic powers enjoyed by certain businesses, tariff and quota restrictions were phased out.

- Existing notions on "economic size" were challenged. Businesses no longer had to confirm to a particular pre-decided size. Anyone could produce and sell whatever quantities of products that they were able to manufacture.
- Industry structure too altered radically in many businesses, forcing players to change gear. Quality products and services entered the market. Supply started overtaking demand. Hence, many industries which were lax had to gear up for the changes.
- Economic Darwinism became the order. "Survival of the fittest" became the new corporate mantra for success. The companies or industries which were able to withstand the competitive forces[1] emerged successfully and others had to follow suit. The companies which did not change or improve vanished from the scene.

The MNC Onslaught:

- With majority equity stake for the parent MNCs, their Indian subsidiaries gained a new strategic advantage. Indian subsidiaries of MNCs gained technological and strategic advantage from their respective parent companies.
- MNCs also gained majority equity stake in their joint ventures with Indian firms and started controlling the show.
- However, Indian companies also faced the takeover threat from MNCs.
- An overall unequal battle between struggling Indian companies and overbearing MNCs went on for some time.

The all pervasive competition:

- Companies faced competition from Indian players, MNCs and imports.
- Technology became easily available and many Indian companies took this opportunity to buy advanced technology from abroad. This gave rise to competition on account of easier access to technology.
- Ultimately, competition became global in character so that Indian companies were no longer competing amongst each other, but with the entire world.

The exacting demands of a buyers' market:

- The Indian economy saw a transition from being a shortage economy to a surplus economy; so the new challenge was to be price competitive.
- Overall, the market model changed from being a sellers' market to being a buyers' market. This caused sharp change in business style.
- The markets saw a change in quality of products--From shoddy products to excellent products.

The new compulsion to find export markets:

- The new trade policy, linking of imports to exports and market driven exchange rate, constituted the main compulsion. Since, India largely remains an import driven economy, the balance of payments deficit always remains a matter of concern. Opening up of the economy brought in a plethora of imported goods into the economy which needed to be balanced out with exports.
- Heat of competition at home was another compulsion why Indian industries had to find export markets.
- However, exporting still remains a difficult game. Indian Exporters are many a time unable to meet the quality requirements of the western countries. Bureaucratic hurdles, red-tapism and complex foreign exchange transactions further complicate exports.
- India's lack of competitiveness as a nation compounds the problem.

Challenges on the technological front:

- Competitive advantage and core competence became technology based.
- Investment in R&D and innovation became inescapable.

Corporate Vulnerability:

Indian companies were by and large vulnerable.

A variety of factors have led to vulnerability; they are:

- Indian companies faced the problem of Capital inadequacy. The financial system was not as robust and availability of credit was scarce.
- Another major problem which Indian companies faced was the lack of product clout and brand power. Indian brands did not have international recognition and quality of Indian products was not considered in very high regard the world over.

- Public Sector units faced a variety of problems such as inefficiency, obsolete technology, lack of professional management, improper utilization of assets and resources etc.
- Indian companies faced the problem of "one product syndrome." One company made only one product; most companies did not have a wide product range.
- Indian companies had to face the problem of loss of monopoly. The protection which they were earlier getting was no longer available and they had to bear the onslaught of foreign and domestic competition.

Discontinuity of the economic trends:

- Past ceased to be an indication of the future. Since, the whole economic environment changed from largely socialistic to emerging capitalistic, the past industry norms, trends and figures held no meaning and were rendered useless for future reference.
- It was no longer business as usual. There was rampant widespread change in every aspect of business.
- Companies were faced with the problem of managing mega change; there was an urgent need for new approaches, new systems and structures, new leadership.

These were some of the major environmental changes which happened in the Indian business environment post liberalization. Indian companies had no option but to gear up for the onslaught of world class products and services from multinational companies. Either grow or perish became the new corporate slogan. There are two ways to achieve growth. Either, to grow organically, by expanding capacity and increasing production, broadening the product line, capturing new markets etc., or, to grow inorganically through the merger route. In the latter option, an existing company takes over or merges another existing company with itself. This method has several advantages, the foremost being the speed of growth. Merging an ongoing business with itself is much easier than increasing capacity from scratch. Mergers also lead to operating and financial synergies, technological upgradation through technology transfers, increase in market share, increase in product breadth and advantages of large size.

In the corporate world, competition is an inevitable part of business. In this scenario if a firm wants to survive then it should have sustainable competitive advantage. According to Michael Porter there are two basic types of competitive advantages that a firm can possess: *low cost* or *differentiation*. If the firm goes ahead with differentiation then it basically selects one or more attributes that many buyers perceive as important and then it uniquely positions itself to meet those needs of the buyers. The firm in return for the uniqueness gets the premium price. If the firm adopts low cost then it tries to achieve the status of low cost producer in its industry. The firm becomes a cost leader due to economies of scale, proprietary technology or any other factors. The firm should focus on its generic strategy whether it is differentiation or it is cost leadership. The core of a firm's strategic plan should be its generic strategy. The strategy that the firm adopts will then lead to competitive advantage. Mergers, acquisitions or other types of restructuring activities are by themselves not strategies but means to achieve strategy. Since every business wants to grow, mergers and acquisitions are innate to this goal.

Organic growth is the internal growth initiated by the company. Organic growth is not always practical since it takes time to install new capacity or to develop new products or services. Technology upgradation and getting the right type of personnel for the job is also not easy. So in order to grow at a faster pace, a company may resort to *inorganic growth* i.e., through the merger or acquisition route. When time is the essence then it may become imperative to resort to inorganic growth route. This throws some light on the fact that M&A activity has become quite common and also the need of the hour for some of the industries and corporates.

[1] Five Competitive forces of Michael Porter namely Threat of New Entrants, Bargaining power of suppliers, Bargaining power of Buyers, Threat of Substitutes and Interfirm rivalry.

CHAPTER SIX

Trends in the Indian Mergers and Acquisitions Scenario (2001-2010)

Indian activities in the arena of mergers and acquisitions have indeed increased manifold over the last one decade. According to India Brand Equity Foundation, the trust run by the Union Ministry of Commerce and Confederation of Indian Industry (CII), outward investment to the tune of $80 billion has been made between the years 2000 and 2010; the UK and the US have emerged as the favoured destinations.

A CII survey report shows that Indian companies actually helped save and create thousands of jobs in the US through acquisitions of local firms there. It reports that since the year 2005, nearly 65 per cent of the Indian companies operating in the US have added jobs to their operations; more than 80 per cent of the hiring was local.

Some of the significant M&A deals involving Indian companies during the period 2001-2010:

THE TATA GROUP

In February, year 2000, The Tetley Group, the world's second largest producer and distributor of tea, was purchased by India's Tata Group for British £ 271 million.

In the year 2004, Tata Motors acquired Daewoo's truck manufacturing unit in South Korea.

In the year 2005, Tata Motors acquired 21 per cent of Aragonese Hispano Carrocera giving it controlling rights of the company.

In January, year 2007, Tata Steel purchased a 100 per cent stake in the Corus Group at 608 pence per share in an all cash deal, cumulatively valued at US $12.04 billion, fending off a serious challenge from CSN, the Brazilian steel maker. The deal marked the largest Indian takeover of a foreign company and made Tata Steel the world's fifth-largest steel group.

In June, year 2008, Tata Motors acquired British Jaguar Land Rover (JLR), which includes the Daimler and Lanchester brand names, from Ford for US $2.3 billion.

In April, year 2011, Tata Chemicals acquired a 25.1 per cent stake in an ammonia-urea fertiliser complex in Gabon for US $ 290 million in which Singapore-based agro-product processor and supplier Olam International owns a 63 per cent stake and the Republic of Gabon holds 12 per cent. The company acquired the stake as a strategic investor and is likely to invest another US $ 170 million in the second phase of expansion of the fertiliser complex.

ADITYA BIRLA GROUP

In February, year 2007, the Aditya Birla Group's Hindalco entered into an agreement to acquire Canadian company Novelis for US $ 6 billion, making the combined entity the world's largest rolled-aluminium producer.

The Group also owns copper mines in the Great Sandy Desert, Western Australia and the Mt. Isa Block in Queensland.

UB GROUP

United Spirits Ltd (USL), the flagship of the UB group and the world's third largest spirits producer, purchased the Scottish distiller Whyte and Mackay in May, year 2007 for British £ 595 million. This included brands like The Dalmore, Isle of Jura, Glayva, Fettercairn, Vladivar Vodka and Whyte & Mackay Scotch.

In the year 2006, Asian Opportunities and Investments Limited, UB's wholly owned subsidiary in Mauritius, announced the acquisition of French wine maker Bouvet Ladubay for € 14.75 million.

BHARTI GROUP

The US $ 10.7 billion acquisition of Zain's African business by Bharti Airtel in the year 2010 was the second largest ever involving an Indian company.

ONGC

In January, year 2009, ONGC Videsh Limited (OVL) completed the acquisition of Imperial Energy Corporation Plc, a UK-based company having exploration and production assets in Tomsk region of Western Siberia, Russia, with an investment of over US $ 2.1billion.

SUZLON ENERGY

In March, year 2006, Hansen Transmissions, the Belgian gearbox maker for wind turbines, was acquired by the Tulsi Tanti-led wind turbine major, Suzlon Energy, through its subsidiary, AE-Rotor Holding BV, for € 465 million in cash.

In May, year 2007, a series of protracted bidding resulted in Suzlon Energy acquiring the majority shareholding in Repower, the German wind turbine manufacturer, for € 1.3 billion. Suzlon subsequently strengthened its position by buying another 30 per cent stake in June, 2008, for more than € 350 million. In 2009, Suzlon raised its share to 92 per cent of Repower.

MAHINDRA & MAHINDRA

In January, year 2007, Mahindra and Mahindra Limited, through its Mauritius-based subsidiary Mahindra Forgings Global Limited, acquired a 90.47 per cent stake in Schoneweiss & Co. GmbH., a leading company in the forgings sector in Germany and valued at € 90 million then. The value of the deal was not disclosed

Meanwhile, foreign companies were also busy in snapping up Indian companies as and when they smelt opportunities. Here are a few most notable ones.

VODAFONE

In the year 2007, Vodafone Group bought out the 33 per cent stake of Essar Group for US $ 5 billion in Hutchison Essar. Earlier on February 11, 2007, Vodafone had agreed to acquire the controlling interest of 67 per cent held by Li Ka Shing Holdings in Hutchison-Essar for US $ 11.1 billion.

DAIICHI-SANKYO

In June, year 2008, Daiichi-Sankyo of Japan acquired a 34.8 per cent stake in Ranbaxy for US $ 2.4 billion. In November, 2008, the Japanese drugs major completed the takeover in a deal worth US $ 4.6 billion by acquiring a 63.92 per cent stake in Ranbaxy.

HOLCIM

A 67 per cent stake in Ambuja Cement India Limited was acquired by Holcim, the Swiss-based cement and construction materials giant, for US $ 634.9 million.

IBM

The year 2004 deal involving the acquisition of Business Process Outsourcing service provider Daksh e-Services by technology behemoth IBM was valued between US $ 130 million and US $ 170 million.

Mergers and acquisitions have become the accepted way to grow business in today's world. It is less time-consuming than greenfield projects and the higher cost is compensated by technology transfer and instant market access.

Table No. 8 - A snapshot of the Major Merger Deals involving Indian Companies (2007-2010)

Rank	M&A Deals 2007 to 2010	Deal Value (US $ Billion)	Sector	Year of Transaction
1	CORUS – Tata Steel	12.2	Steel	2007
2	RELIANCE NATURAL – Reliance Power	11.0	Oil and Gas	2010
3	HUTCHISON – Vodafone	10.8	Telecom	2007
4	ZAIN – Bharti	10.7	Telecom	2010
5	NOVELIS – Hindalco	6.0	Aluminium	2007
6	RANBAXY – Daiichi Sankyo	4.5	Pharmaceuticals	2009
7	PIRAMAL – Abbott	3.7	Pharmaceuticals	2010
8	IMPERIAL – ONGC Videsh	2.8	Oil and Gas	2008
9	TATA TELE – NTT Docoma	2.7	Telecom	2008
10	CENTURION BANK – HDFC Bank	2.4	Banking and Financial Services	2008

(Source: Grant Thornton Deal tracker 2010)

Total Number of Indian M&A Deals (2000-2011):

The decade from year 2000 to the year 2010 has been very important for the Indian M&As. In the year 2000, the total number of mergers was 186, acquisitions was 173 and the total deals which amounted to takeover of ownership were 225.

The consecutive year 2001 saw lesser number of deals in all the three categories. The number of acquisitions reduced to 121, mergers reduced to 145 from 186 the previous year and takeover of ownership deals reduced to 180 from 225 of the year 2000.

In the years 2002, 2003 and 2004 there were 92, 113 and 79 acquisitions, 178, 149 and 152 mergers and 214, 243 and 246 takeover of ownership deals respectively. From the year 2005 onwards, there was a steep increase in Mergers and Acquisitions in India.

The year 2007 was a benchmark year for mergers and acquisitions in India wherein the maximum number of deals were recorded. The total number of mergers was 172, number of acquisitions was 136 and total takeover of assets deals were 428. After 2007, there was a decline in the number of deals as 2008 was a year of global recession and M&As also faced the brunt of the slump.

In the year 2009, the total number of mergers and acquisition deals was 235 and takeover of ownership number was 234. In the year 2010, the number of takeover deals rose sharply to 214.

The year 2011 has seen tremendous momentum in M&A activity. A record 196 ownership takeover deals have been struck in the first seven months of the year.

Chart No. 5 - Total Number of Indian M&A Deals (2000- July 2011)

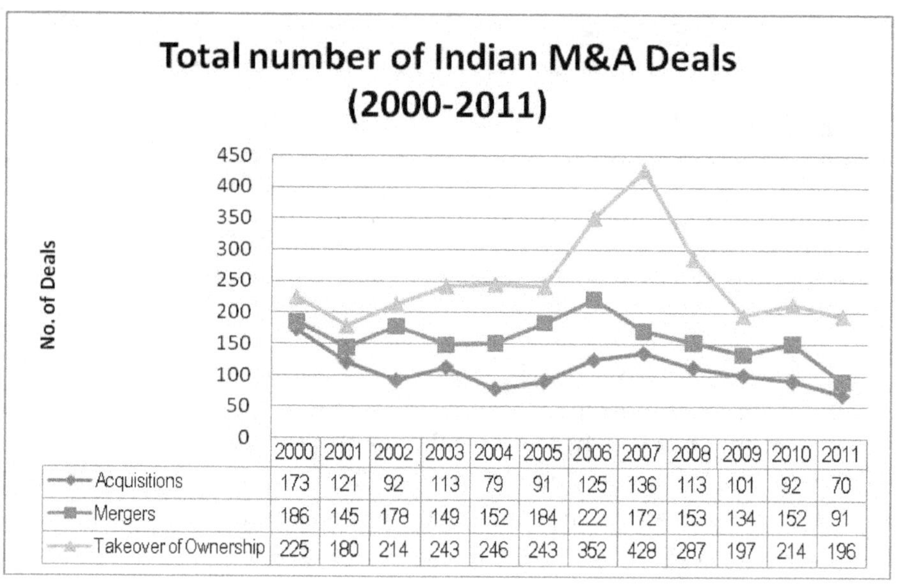

	2000	2001	2002	2003	2004	2005	2006	2007	2008	2009	2010	2011
Acquisitions	173	121	92	113	79	91	125	136	113	101	92	70
Mergers	186	145	178	149	152	184	222	172	153	134	152	91
Takeover of Ownership	225	180	214	243	246	243	352	428	287	197	214	196

(Source: Compiled from Prowess Database 3.1, accessed on 26 July 2011)

In terms of number of acquisitions, there was a 37.4 per cent increase from the year 2005. Infact, the increase started from the year 2005, which posted a 15 per cent growth from the previous year.

There was an increase upto the year 2007, after which the year 2008 saw 16 per cent decrease in Acquisitions due to recessionary global conditions. After that, there was a percentage decline in the number of deals upto the year 2010.

Inbound and Outbound M&A deals

Inbound deals are the deals in which an Indian company (domestic company) takes over or merges with a domestic company whereas an outbound deals is one where in a domestic company takes over a foreign company.

Chart No. 6 - Inbound Vs Outbound M&A Deal Value(2001-2010)

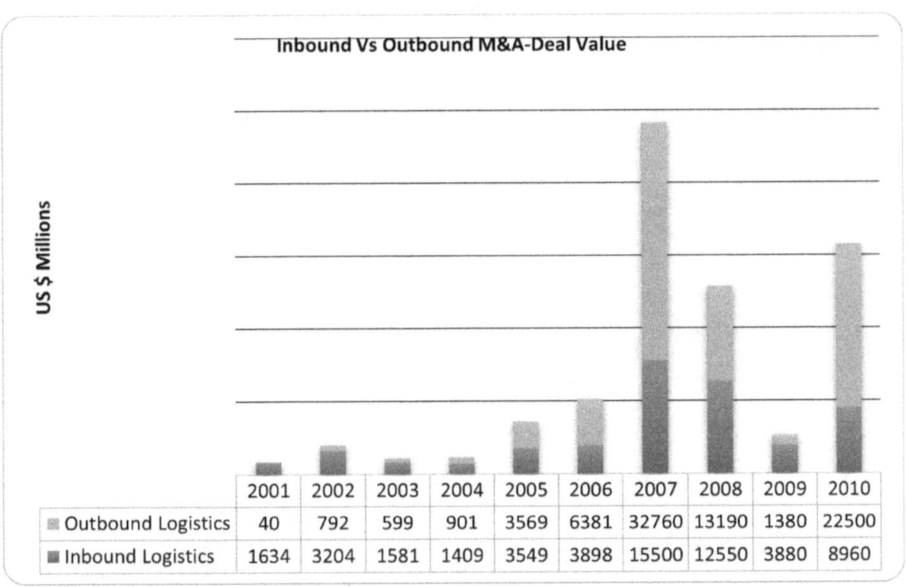

	2001	2002	2003	2004	2005	2006	2007	2008	2009	2010
Outbound Logistics	40	792	599	901	3569	6381	32760	13190	1380	22500
Inbound Logistics	1634	3204	1581	1409	3549	3898	15500	12550	3880	8960

(Source: Compiled from Prowess Database 3.1)

The above chart shows the inbound and outbound merger and acquisition transactions between the years 2001 and 2010. The volume of deals in the year 2007 surpasses all the other years. The volume of inbound and outbound deals in the year 2010 was also remarkable. The inbound deal volume in 2007 was US $ 32,760 million and the volume of inbound deals was around US $ 15500 million. It can be said that the Indian corporate sector was on a outbound shopping spree! Similarly in the year 2010, the volume of outbound deals was US $ 22500 million.

Total Cross Border M&A Activity (2001-2010)

The following is the chart for the cross border M&A activity between the years 2001 and 2010. The year 2007 saw the maximum value of deals which reached close to US $ 50000 millions. After that in the year 2010, the deal value reached close to US $ 35000 millions. The year 2008 was the year of the great financial crises and hence it can be observed that there was a big dip in the M&A activity in the years 2008 and 2009. The total cross border activity of Indian Companies can be seen from the chart below:

Chart No. 7 - Total Cross Border M&A Activity (2001-2010)

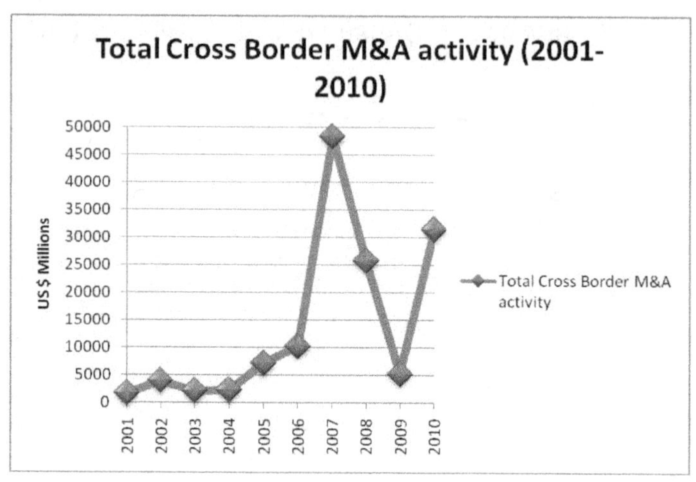

(Source: KPMG Research Report on M&A)

Chart No. 8 - Total M&A Activity in terms of Inbound, Outbound and Domestic Deals (volume and value) (2005-2010)

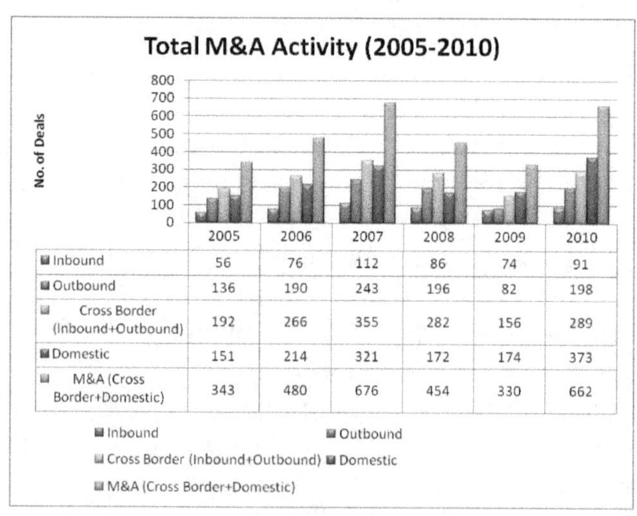

(Source: Compiled from Grant Thornton Research Report-Deal Tracker 2007, 2010)

The year 2007 was very important for Mergers and Acquisitions in India.

There were more than 650 deals in the year 2007, as compared to 480 in the year 2006 and 343 deals in the year 2005. In the year 2008, the number of cross border deals fell to 282 and the domestic deals were around 172. In the year 2009, the M&A (Cross border + Domestic) deals were 330 which again rose to 662 in the year 2010.

There were 13 M&A deals with deal value of over US $500 Mn in the year 2007 as compared to 8 deals and 7 deals in the years 2006 and 2005 respectively.

The value of Cross Border deals (both Inbound and Outbound) announced in the year 2007 had almost tripled from the year 2006. The value of inbound deals increased from $5.1 billion in the year 2005 to US $ 5.4 billion in the year 2006 to US $15.5 billion in the year 2007 and value of outbound deals increased from US $4.3 billion in the year 2005 to US $9.9 billion in the year 2006 to US $32.8 billion in the year 2007.

Tata-Corus, Vodafone-Hutch and Hindalco-Novelis deals accounted for 56.80 per cent of total M&A deals during the year 2007.

The value of domestic deals announced declined from US $ 6.9 billion in the year 2005 to US $ 4.99 billion in the year 2006 to US $ 2.85 billion in the year 2007, even though the volume of domestic deals increased from 151 deals in the year 2005 to 214 deals in the year 2006 to 321 deals in the year 2007.

Though volume of M&A deals grew by 40.83 per cent during the year 2007 as compared to the year 2006, value of M&A deals grew by an astounding 152 per cent.

The total number of M&A Deals announced during the calendar year 2007 was 676 with a total announced value of US $51.12 billion (Private Equity deals have not been accounted for) as against 480 deals with a total announced value of US $ 20.30 billion in the year 2006.

There were 321 domestic deals (both acquirer and target being Indian) with an announced value of US $ 2.85 billion and 355 cross-border deals with an announced value of US $48.26 billion. 243 of the cross border deals were outbound deals (Indian companies acquiring businesses outside India) with a value of US $32.76 billion and 112 were inbound deals (international companies or their subsidiaries acquiring Indian businesses) with an announced value of close to US $15.5 billion.

The average M&A deal value was US $75.61 Million during the year 2007. The average value of cross-border deals (both inbound and outbound) was US $136 Million which was significantly higher when compared to average value of domestic deals which was close to US $ 9 Million.

Chart No. 9 - Total M&A Value (2005-2010)

Total M&A Value (2005-2010)

US $ Billions

	2005	2006	2007	2008	2009	2010
Inbound	5.17	5.4	15.5	12.55	3.88	8.96
Outbound	4.30	9.91	32.76	13.19	1.38	22.5
Cross Border (Inbound+Outbound)	9.47	15.31	48.26	25.74	5.26	31.46
Domestic	6.85	4.99	2.85	5.21	6.7	18.32
M&A (Cross Border+Domestic)	16.32	20.3	51.11	30.95	11.96	49.78

Inbound Outbound Cross Border (Inbound+Outbound) Domestic M&A (Cross Border+Domestic)

(Source: Compiled from Grant Thornton Research Report-Deal Tracker 2007, 2010)

In the year 2008, the total value of M&A deals was around US $ 31 billion which further fell to US $ 11.96 billion in the year 2009.

The year 2010 was again a golden year for M&A in India, with total domestic deals worth US $ 18.32 billion and total M&A deals worth almost US $ 50 billion.

Chart No. 10 - Comprehensive Valuewise, Dealwise and Volumewise Quarterly (2006-2010)

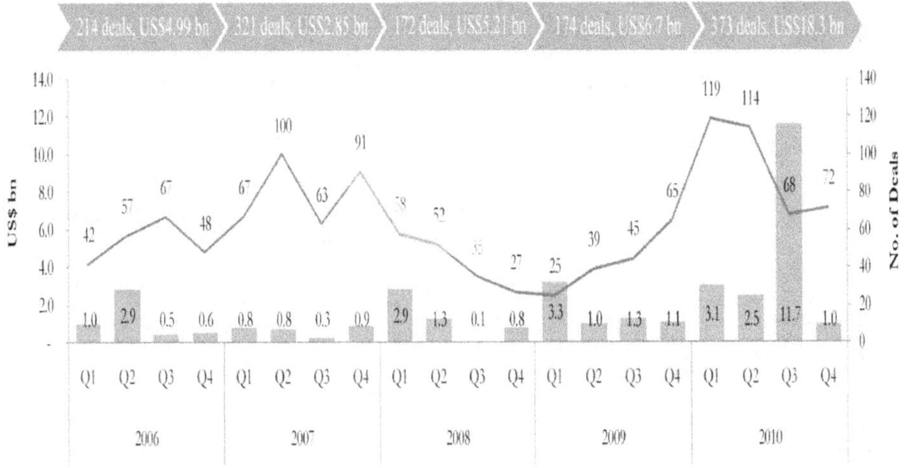

(Source: Grant Thornton Deal tracker 2010) (Q1 ,Q2, Q3, Q4
represents the four quarters in a year)

Characteristics of deals which took place in the year 2007:
It can be seen that the year 2007 was a very important year for M&A in India. The maximum number of deasl took place in the year 2007. The total value of these deals was close to US $ 69 Billion. The following are certain important facts and figure about deals which took place in the year 2007.

Historically, sectors like Automotive, IT, Pharma, Banking sectors etc. were the leading players in M&A. However, the year 2007 saw significant participation by sectors such as Commodities (which primarily comprised Steel, Aluminium and Metals & Ores), Telecom, Power & Energy, Real Estate & Infrastructure.

Steel and Telecom sectors were the clear leaders as far as sectoral values were concerned. These sectors accounted for US $14.9 billion and US $ 11.3 billion worth of deals respectively. Together, they accounted for as much as 51 per cent of the total M&A deal value during the year 2007 and more than the total announced value of M&A deals in the year 2006.

Tata Steel's acquisition of Corus for US $ 12.2 billion and Vodafone's majority stake in Hutchison Essar for US $10.83 billion were the major deals in these sectors.

The steel sector encountered a deal value of about US $ 14,897 million in the year 2007 and the total number of deals was 20. Telecom sector was a close second at US $ 11,333 million with a deal volume of 11. There were totally 676 deals in the year 2007 with an approximate deal value of US $ 51,112 million.

Table No. 9 - Sector wise break up of M&A Transactions in the year 2007

Final Sector	Value (US $ Million)	Percentage deal value	Volume (No. of Deals)	Percentage deal volume
Aluminium	6,000.00	11.74	4	0.59
Automotive	815.97	1.60	31	4.59
Breweries & Distilleries	1,123.43	2.20	6	0.89
Cement	632.87	1.24	8	1.18
Electricals & Electronics	739.56	1.45	11	1.63
IT & ITeS	2,885.58	5.65	159	23.52
Metals & Ores	1,260.54	2.47	10	1.48
Oil & Gas	1,297.97	2.54	16	2.37
Pharma, Healthcare & Biotech	1,465.75	2.87	64	9.47
Power & Energy	3,807.35	7.45	20	2.96
Steel	14,897.62	29.15	20	2.96
Telecom	11,333.28	22.17	11	1.63
Others	4,852.54	9.49	316	46.75
Grand Total	**51,112.47**	**100**	**676**	**100**

(Source: Grant Thornton Deal tracker 2007)

The percentage deal volume and number of deals were maximum in the IT sector however, from the point of view of deal value, the steel sector was the front runner followed closely by the telecom sector.

The aluminium sector saw deals worth US $ 6000 million and power and energy sector had deals worth close to US $ 4000 million.

The IT sector was fifth in terms of deal value but first in terms of number of deals. A total of 159 deals were done in the IT sector. Pharma and healthcare was second with 64 deals and the automotive sector was third with 31 deals in total.

Chart No. 11 - Sector wise break up of M&A Transactions in 2007 (Volume)

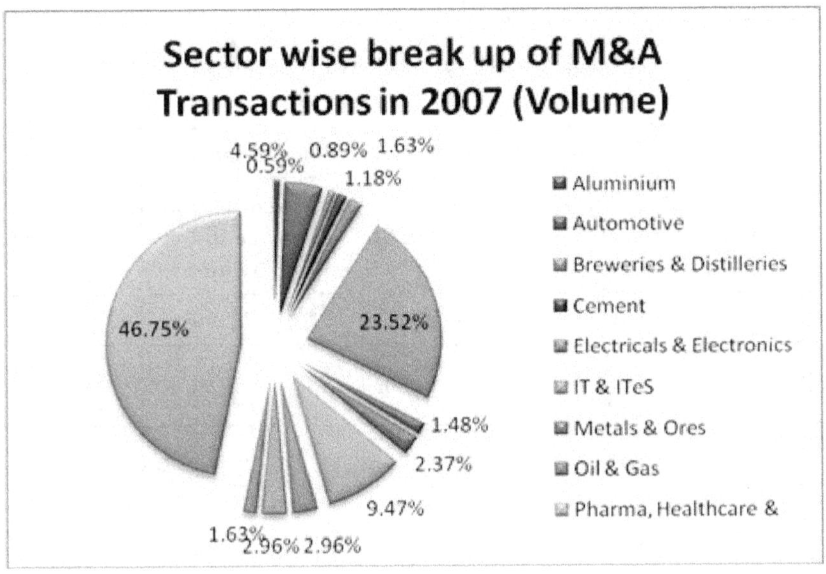

(Source: Grant Thornton Deal tracker 2007)

Chart No. 12 - Sector wise break up of M&A Transactions in 2007 (Value)

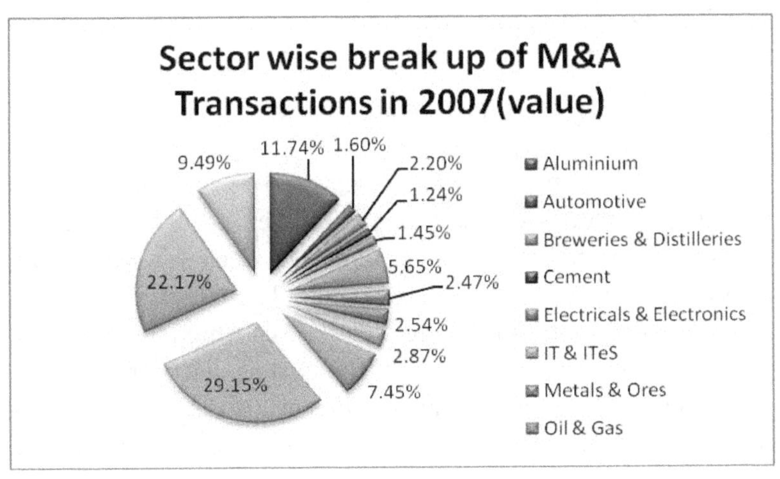

(Source: Grant Thornton Deal tracker 2007)

The above chart shows the percentage wise value of M&A deals of different sectors in the year 2007.

Table No. 10 - Billion Dollar Plus M&A Deals in the year 2007

Billion Dollar Plus M&A Deals in 2007				
Acquirer	**Target**	**Sector**	**Acquisition price in US $ Millions**	**Deal Type**
Tata Steel	Corus	Steel	12,201.6	Acquisition
Vodafone	Hutchison Essar	Telecom	10,830.00	Majority Stake
Hindalco Industries	Novelis Inc.	Aluminum	6,000.00	Acquisition
Suzlon Energy Ltd	REpower	Power & Energy	1,700.93	Controlling Stake
Essar Steel Holdings	Algoma Steel Inc.	Steel	1,580.00	Acquisition
United Spirits Ltd	Whyte & Mackay	Breweries & Distilleries	1,112.99	Acquisition
Tata Power	PT Kaltim Prima Coal	Power & Energy	1,100.00	Significant Stake

(Source: Grant Thornton Deal Tracker 2007)

There were 7 "billion dollar" M&A deals in the year 2007 compared to none in the year 2006. India Inc also witnessed a lesser number of low value deals as compared to previous years. The deals for which value was not disclosed were typically small sized deals. The largest deals of the year 2007 were Tata-Corus and Vodafone-Hutch deals which were completed in early part of the year 2007 – making it the perfect start for a year of M&A transactions. Of the 7 "billion dollar" deals, 3 deals were in the metal sector, 2 deals in Power & Energy and 1 deal each in Telecom and Breweries & Distilleries sectors. Together, these 7 "billion dollar" deals accounted for 67.47 percentage of total M&A during the year 2007. Hence, the year 2007 can be considered an important year for understanding different nuances of M&A deals.

Characteristics of deals which took place in the year 2010:

The year 2010 was also a significant year for M&As in India. After the year 2007, the year 2010 recorded the highest value deals close to around US $ 67 Billion. The following are some of the characteristics of deals which took place in the year 2010.

Chart No. 13- M&A Activities in India (2010)

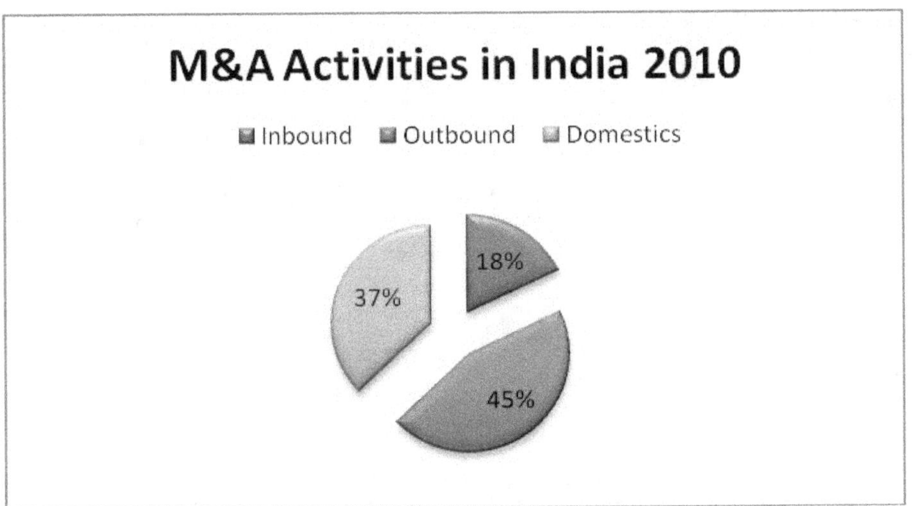

(Source: Grant Thornton Research)

In the year 2010, the maximum volume of deals took place in the Oil and Gas Sector crossing a value of US $ 11,000 million. The next in line was the telecom sector at US $ 3093 million. Real estate and Banking were at US $ 834.38 million and US $ 711.17 million respectively.

IIn terms of volume, the banking sector had the maximum number of deals in the year 2010. Pharma and healthcare sector came in second at 27 deals. Oil and Gas sector had only 8 deals which accounted for the highest value. The total number of real estate deals came to be 26 which was the the third most important sector in terms of the number of deals. Total number of deals in the metals and ores sector was 20. There were several deals in FMCG sector amounting to around US $ 256 million. Several big ticket deals took place in hospitality, pharma and healthcare, power and energy and aviation too.

Chart No. 14 - M&A Deals by Industry in 2010

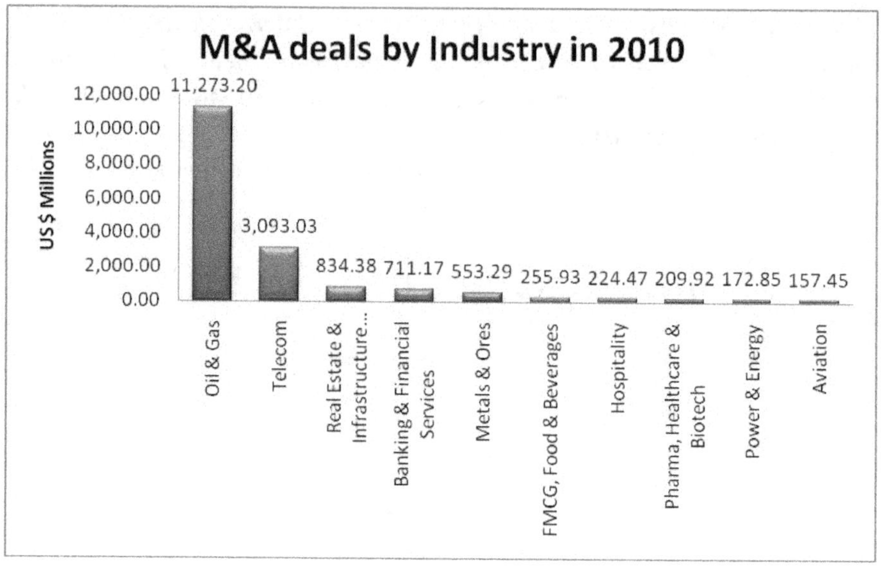

(Source: Grant Thornton Deal Tracker 2010)

Chart No. 15 - M&A Deals by Industry in 2010 (Volume)

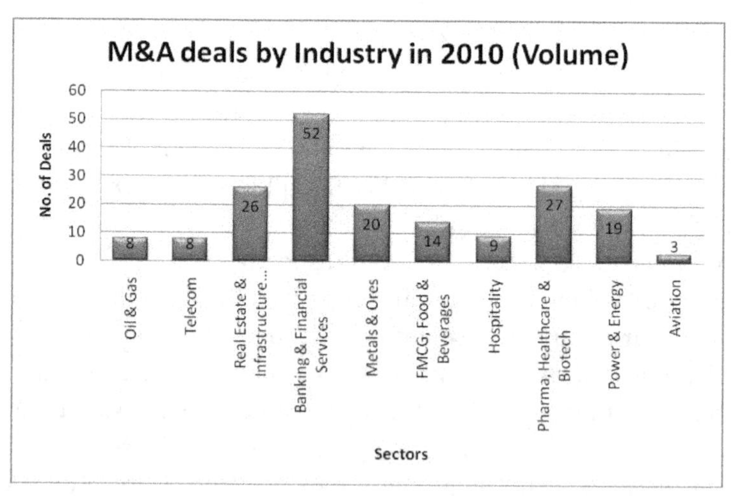

(Source: Grant Thornton Deal Tracker 2010)

Chart No. 16 - Sector wise Percentage Share in Total M&A (2010)

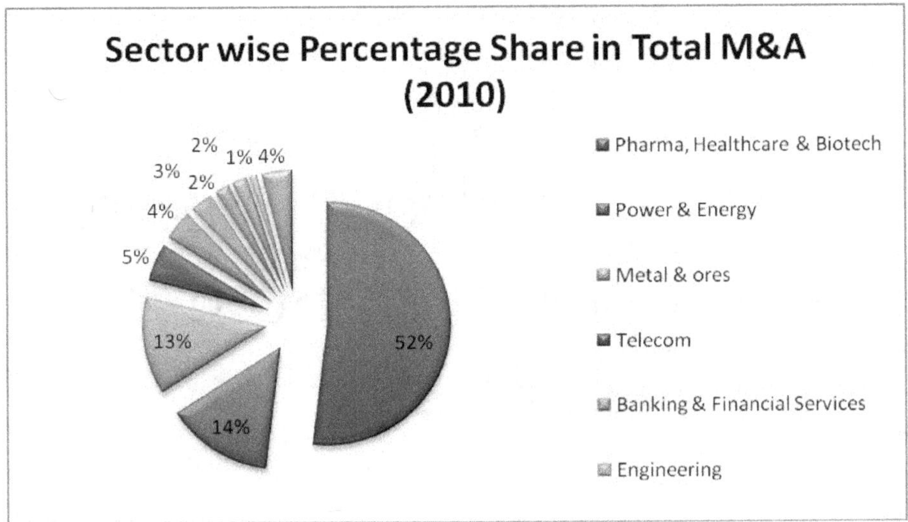

(Source: Grant Thornton Deal Tracker 2010)

The pharmaceutical and healthcare sector had the highest 52 percentage share in the total M&A in the year 2010. The Power and Energy sector had a 14 percentage share in the total deals and Metals and Ores sector had a 13 percentage share. Out of all the deals which took place in the year 2010, 45 percentage were outbound M&As, 37 percentage were domestic deals and the remaining were inbound deals.

The increasing confidence in the Indian Economy, buoyancy in the Capital markets, significant improvements in global perception of India and improved performance of the cross border transactions, resulted in the increased M&A activity in India. Opportunities across sectors in India have continued to fuel M&A activity. The increasing need for telecom infrastructure, oil & gas, primary & tertiary healthcare and power sectors ensured both growth and consolidation related transactions within these sectors. Cross border activity also surged significant outbound investments have taken place.

CHAPTER SEVEN

Trends in the Indian Mergers and Acquisitions Scenario (2010-2020)

Over 500,000 merger and acquisition (M&A) deals have been completed globally since 2010. The yearly figure fluctuated since, but increased overall, exceeding 63,000 during 2021. Goldman Sachs, JPMorgan, and Morgan Stanley advised on the largest number of M&A deals.

Table No. 11 - A snapshot of the Major Merger Deals involving Indian Companies (2020)

Acquirer	Target	Sector	USD billion	Deal type	%Stake
Facebook inc	Jio platforms Ltd.	Telecom	5700	Minority Stake	10%
Google LIC	Jio platforms Ltd.	Telecom	4439	Minority Stake	8%
Reliance Retail Venture Ltd.	The future group retail and wholesale business	Retail and consumer	3295	Acquisition	100%
Holdia Petrochemical limited	Lummus technology LIC	Energy and natural resources	1544	Controlling Stake	57%
Adani ports and special economic zone L limited	Krishnapatnam Port Company Ltd.	Transport and Logistics	1434	Majority stake	75%
SBI, HDFC ,KOTAK MAHINDRA, AXISBANK,IDFC BANK	YES Bank Ltd.	Banking and financial services	1389	Majority Stake	N.A
Group Aeroports De Paris sa	GMR airport holding Ltd.	Infrastructure management	1369	Strategic Stake	49%
Embassy office Parks REIT	Embassy group	Real estate	1322	Acquisition	100%
Walmart Inc.	Flipkart online services Pvt. Ltd.	E- commerce	1200	Minority Stake	N.A
NTPC LTD.	THDC India Ltd.	Energy and natural resources	1014	Majority Stake	74%

Source: Grant Thornton Deal Tracker

The value of M&A deals worldwide fluctuated significantly since 2010. A peak value of over four trillion U.S. dollars was reached in 2014. Since then, annual deal values have risen and fallen sporadically. In 2015, a value close to the peak value of the time period was reached, after which deal values gradually declined. In 2021, M&A deal value reached approximately 5.9 trillion U.S. dollars.

Chart No. 17 - Total number of M&A Deals Worldwide (2010-2021)

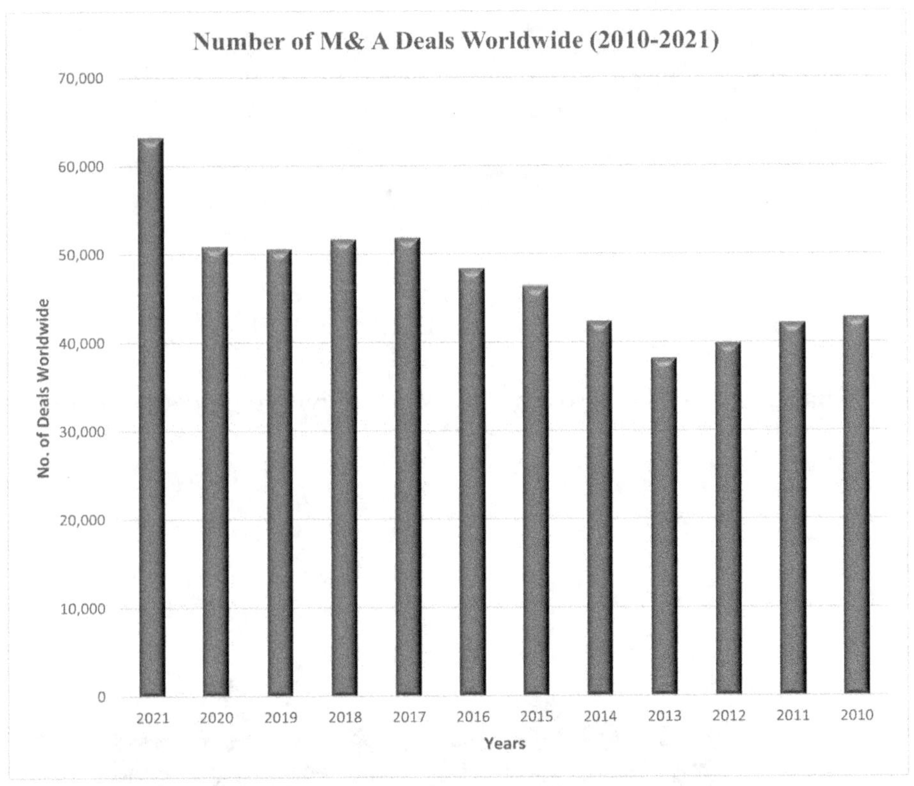

Source: Prowess Database: CMIE

The chart number 18 shows the inbound and outbound merger and acquisition transactions between 2014 to 2019.The volume of deals in the year 2014 surpasses all the other years The inbound value in the year 2014 was US $ 10.4 billion. Outbound deal value at US $12.8 billion in 2018, the year 2019 witnessed an all-time low deal value of US $ 2 billion, 6.4 times fall compared to 2018.

Chart No. 18 - Total number of Inbound and Outbound Deals (2014-2019)

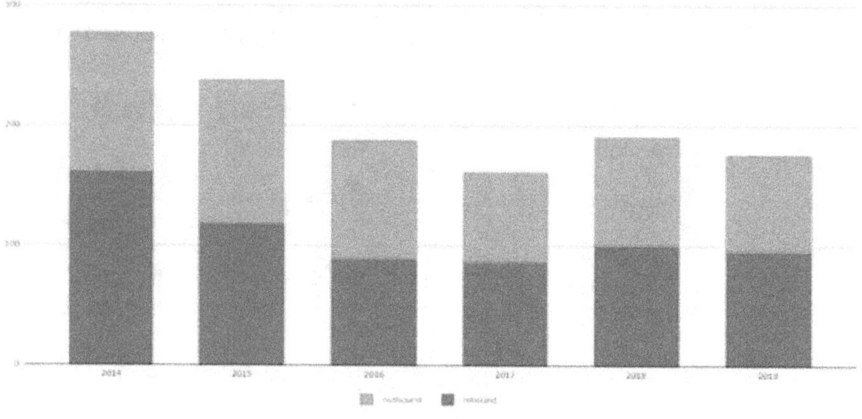

Source: Prowess Database: CMIE

Chart No. 19 - Total cross border M&A activity regionwise (2012 – 2021)

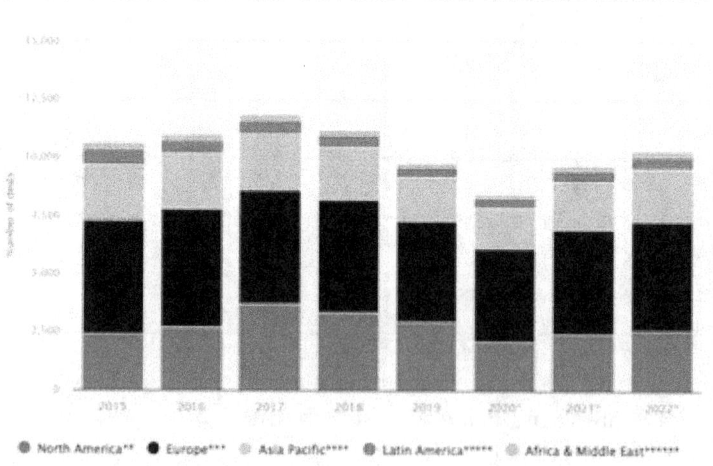

Source: Statista

Chart No. 20 - Deal Volume by Transaction Size (2012-2021)

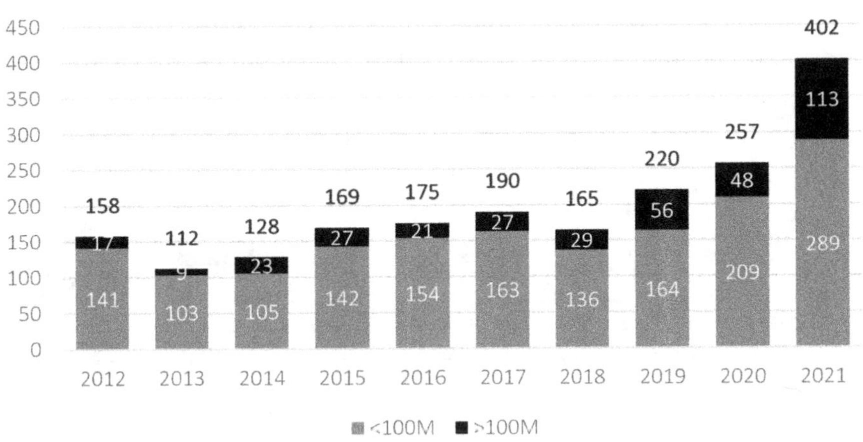

Source: Capitaline Database

Across the sectors, more than 400 deals were announced in 2021, up more than 55% from 257 deals in 2020 and 83% from 220 in 2019.

Chart No. 21 - Comprehensive Value wise and volume wise global deals (2001-2021)

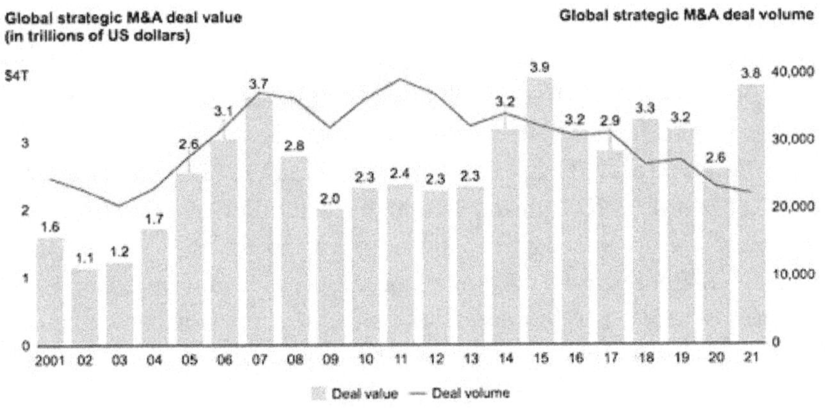

Source: Capitaline Database

The year 2021 brought record-breaking merger & acquisition deal values, with total transaction values reaching an unmatched $5.9 trillion.Globally, 2021 is the strongest opening nine months of M&A since records began. In the U.S. alone, target M&A has surged 139 percent to US$2Tn. So far in 2021, 757 deals worth more than a billion dollars have been announced.

Table No. 12 - Sectorwise breakup of M&A transactions in the year 2021

Sector	Value	%	Volume	%
Start-up	857	2.03	122	25.68
IT & ITES	8511	20.13	78	16.42
E-commmerce	2597	6.14	53	11.16
Pharma health care & biotech	1645	3.89	48	10.11
Manufacturing	3100	7.33	29	6.11
Retail & consumer	678	1.6	29	6.11
Banking & Financial Services	9361	22.14	27	5.68
Education	2935	6.94	23	4.84
Media & Entertainment	741	1.75	23	4.84
Energy & natural resources	7466	17.66	18	3.79
Hospitality & leisure	234	0.55	13	2.74
Telecom	529	1.25	5	1.05
Aviation	2470	5.84	2	0.42
transpport & logistics	1158	2.74	5	1.05

Source: Capitaline Database

As it can be observed from table no. 22, in the year 2021, the highest value of deals happened in the banking and financial services sector. Deals worth Rs. 9361 crore. The total number of deals in the financial services sector amounted to 27. The value of deals in the IT & ITES sector amounted to Rs. 8511 crore with 78 deals. The highest number of deals happened in the start up sector with 122 deals amounting to Rs. 857 crore. The total deal value in Energy and natural resources sector amounted to Rs 7466 crore with 18 deals. Total number of deals in the aviation sector amounted to 2 but the total number of deals in the sector were only 2. This would mean that the deals were of a large ticket size. Total number of deals in Ecommerce sector was 53 and in pharma sector 48.

Chart No. 22 - Sectorwise breakup of M&A transaction in 2021(value)

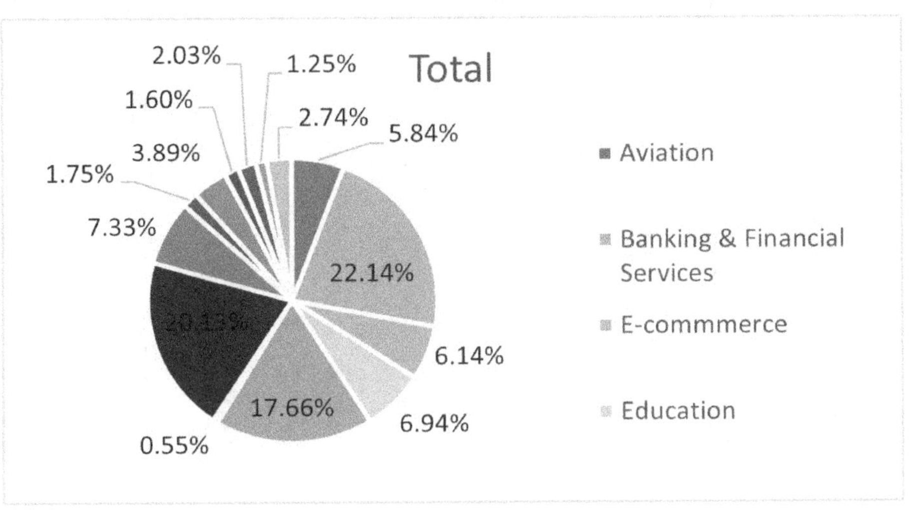

Source: Grant Thornton Deal Tracker (2021)

Chart No. 23 - Sectorwise breakup of M&A transaction in 2021(volume)

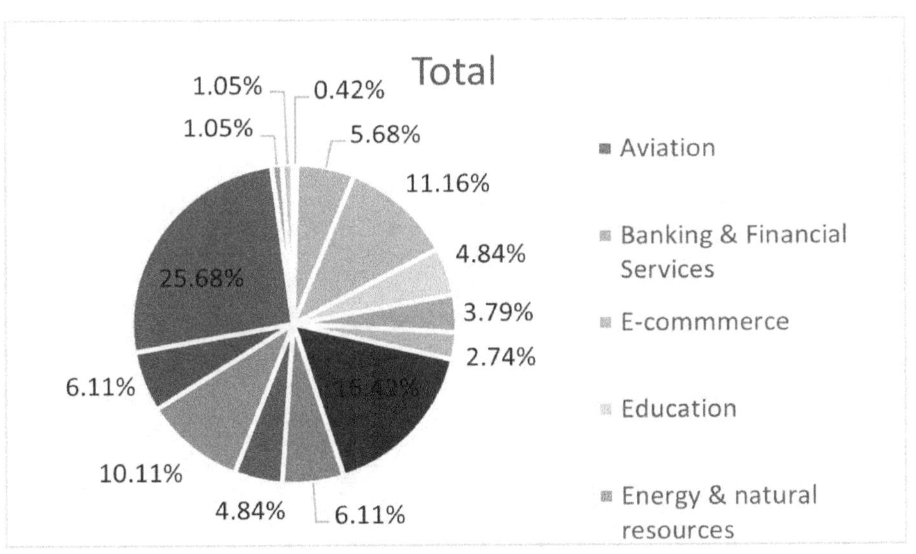

Source: Grant Thornton Deal Tracker (2021)

CHAPTER EIGHT

Economic Activity and M&A

Understanding the relationship between Economic Development and M&A activity:

It has been time and again established that positive economic and financial conditions of a country lead to an increase in M&A activity-Cross border as well as domestic. Berthelemy and Demurger (2000) discuss and confirm the fundamental role played by FDI in economic growth, and stress the importance of the potential for future growth in foreign investment. This line of thinking is also supported by Liu et al. (2009), who observe a two-way causal relationship between trade, inward FDI, inward M&A, and economic growth for most of the economies. It is evident that the presence of economic growth and business trade is a necessary condition for an M&A market to develop. The development of domestic capital markets is a key driver of M&A activity since investment requires capital and it is easier and more cost-effective to source capital from the local market. Therefore, the development of stock markets is of high importance.

(2008) argues that macroeconomic factors such as the income level, gross domestic investment, banking sector development, private capital flows, and stock market liquidity are important determinants of the degree of stock market development in emerging market countries. Saborowski (2009) shows evidence that the exchange rate appreciation effect of FDI inflows is indeed attenuated when financial and capital markets are larger and more active. The main implication of these results is that one of the main dangers associated with large capital inflows in emerging markets – the destabilization of macroeconomic management (due to a sizeable appreciation of the real exchange rate) – can be partly mitigated by developing a deep financial sector. This idea highlights the importance of developed capital markets and a stable financial system to the ability to sustain M&A activity.

Hence, in order to understand the M&A activity in India, the understanding of the Indian Economic scenario during the period of study becomes imperative.

Overview of the Indian Economy:

India is a growing economy with strong fundamentals. As per the statistics of July 2011, India is a US$ 4.002 trillion economy (purchasing power parity) which accounts for a 6.0% share of world income, the fourth largest in the world in terms of real GDP (Report for Selected Countries and Subjects- International Monetary Fund. Accessed on 2011-01-07).

The discussion about the Indian Economy can be broken down into three distinct phases, viz.,

(i) The Post Independence Era (1948-1990),

(ii) The LPG Initiation Phase(1991-1999),

(iii) The post LPG growth phase.

The first two phases have been discussed in brief. A detailed discussion of the third phase ensues.

Post Independence Era:

The post independence period of the economy of India was a challenging phase for the economic planners. Having come out of the shadow of colonial rule, the nation had a huge challenge of undoing the exploitation of the colonial era. The founding fathers had to use economic upliftment as a tool for nation building.

Industry was characterized by ill equipped technology and unscientific management. Agriculture was still feudal in nature and characterized by low productivity. Transport and communication systems were not properly developed, educational and health facilities insufficient and the complete absence of social security measures. Poverty was visible and unemployment widespread, resulting in a low standard of living. To guide the Indian economy towards a path of growth and development, the economic planners decided to adopt a course of mixed economy, assigning a vital role to public sector enterprises and economic planning.

Private enterprise participation was negligible. A system of License Raj developed, by which entrepreneurs had to seek permission from government to set up manufacturing units. The government effectively controlled everything. During this period the banks were nationalized between late 1960's and early 1970's.

India resorted to economic planning by the way of five year plans for economic development.

Table No. 13 - Growth Rates of the Indian Economy Between 1951 And 1990

Period	Growth Rate of NNP	Per capita NNP growth rate
First plan period (1951-56)	3.6	1.8
Second Plan period (1956-61)	4.1	2.0
Third Plan Period (1961-66)	2.5	0.2
Annual Plan (1966-69)	3.8	1.5
Fourth Plan (1969-74)	3.3	1.0
Fifth Plan (1974-79)	5.0	2.7
Annual Plan (1979-80)	-6.0	-8.3
Sixth Plan (1980-85)	5.3	3.1
Seventh Plan (1985-90)	5.9	3.7

(Source: http://www.liberalsindia.com/relevence/IndEconomy.php)

Some Glaring Problems of the Indian Economy (1950-1990):

- Exports registered a sharp decline in this period.
- Large scale demographic problems such as illiteracy, high infant mortality rate, lack of safe drinking water and other sanitation problems, poverty etc., posed great hindrances to the economic growth.
- Structural imbalances and financial problems further weakened the economic system.
- Public sector performed poorly. Instead of generating cash flows in the economy, PSUs ate up the savings of the nation.
- The financial system was not competent with world standards.
- Competition was lacking among the industries.

The crisis of 1990:

By the beginning of 1990's, the Indian Economy was under great crisis and faced its stiffest challenge. India faced a serious balance of payment problem and foreign exchange reserves were at record low.

That is when the government decided to alter the course of the Indian economy. The reforms can be divided into two time frames:

The LPG Initiation Phase:

India freed itself from the shackles of socialistic economics in the year 1991. This became the turning point for the country in terms of industrial and economic development. The Indian economy embraced the three pillars of a free market system, viz., Liberalisation, Privatisation and Globalisation.

The Licensing and MRTP Acts were done away with. This basically relieved the industries from the cumbersome paperwork and bureaucratic formalities which were earlier required. With this breath of fresh air the SME sector started its unprecedented growth story. This in turn worked as a huge support mechanism for the large scale sector.

Privatization brought new hope for the large scale PSUs which were grossly mismanaged. The government has allowed private participation in most of the PSUs and is continuing to do so in a phased manner. Shares of companies such as IPCL, ONGC, Maruti Udhyog Ltd, GAIL, etc., were offered to the public at large and to the private players in order to have a turn around.

The privatization movement took stronghold in the banking sector too and strong banking institutions such as ICICI bank, IDBI bank and HDFC bank came into being. By adopting world class technology, innovative products and highly efficient management, these institutions were able to bring about a revolution in the Indian financial sector. And obviously the biggest beneficiary of a strong financial system is the industry.

Export pessimism and import substitution were the main tenets of the Indian trade policy before the year 1990. But with the onset of globalization, that was about to change. The gulf crisis made us aware that even a relatively closed economy cannot escape foreign exchange crisis.

Improvement in merchandise and invisible exports and modulation of import demand were addressed to. A switch over to market determined exchange rate, building up forex reserves and elimination of the dependence on short term debt were some of the most important changes that were brought about.

Chart No. 24 - The GDP Pre and Post Reforms

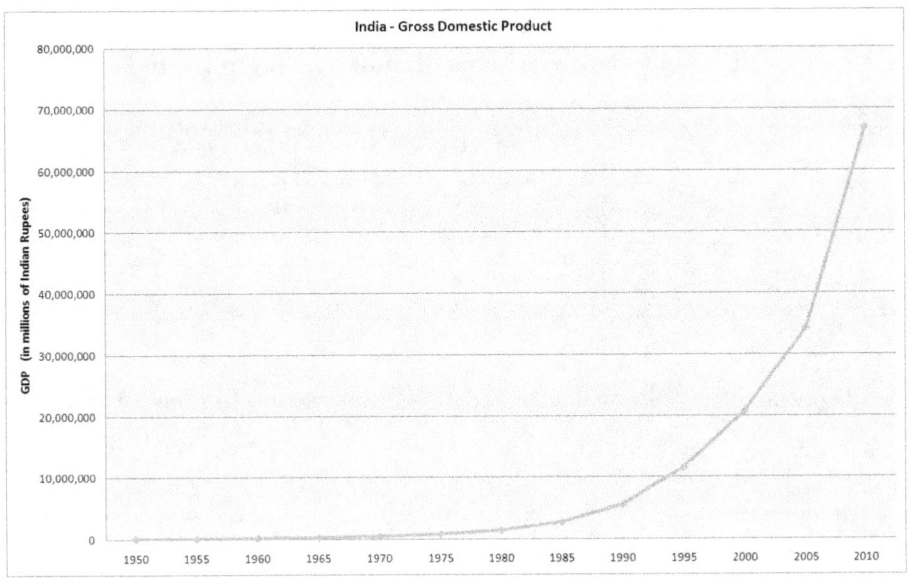

Source: Compiled from World Bank Data (accessed July 2011)

It can be seen from Chart No. 24 that before the 1990s, the GDP was almost stagnant. The reforms introduced after the year 1990 gave a strong boost to the GDP. In the year 1990, it was about 6,00,00,000 Mn. Rupees which increased to about 11,00,00,000 Mn. Rupees in the year 1995 and reached 20,00,00,000 Mn. Rupees in the year 2000.

The Post LPG Growth Phase:

The Indian economy grew by leaps and bounds after the year 2000. The era between the years 1990 and 1999 was the era of destabilization, wide scale economic restructuring and changing competitive scenario for the Indian corporate sector.

This has been discussed in detail earlier. It can be said that the decade 1990-1999 was a settling and acclimatization period for the Indian economy and corporate sector at large. With the dawn of the new millennium, the Indian economy started reaping the fruits of the reforms which were initiated a decade ago.

A growth spurt was seen in all the major macroeconomic parameters which ultimately reflected on the corporate sector of the country.

The Indian economy started growing at a faster pace post the 1991 reforms. By the 12th five year plan, India was showing a consistent growth rate of around 8 percent per annum.

Table No. 14 - Growth Rates of Indian Economy upto 2017

Period	Growth Rate of NNP	Per Capita NNP growth rate
Eighth Plan (1992-97)	6.8	3.4
Ninth Plan (1997-2002)	6.8	3.4
Tenth Plan (2002-07)	7.6	3.8
Eleventh Plan (2007-12)	8	4
Twelfth Plan (2012-17)	8	4

(Source: http://www.liberalsindia.com/relevence/IndEconomy.php)

The Indian economy started growing at a faster pace post the 1991 reforms. By the 12th five year plan, India was showing a consistent growth rate of around 8 percent per annum.

Chart No. 25 - GDP Growth of India (2010-2021)

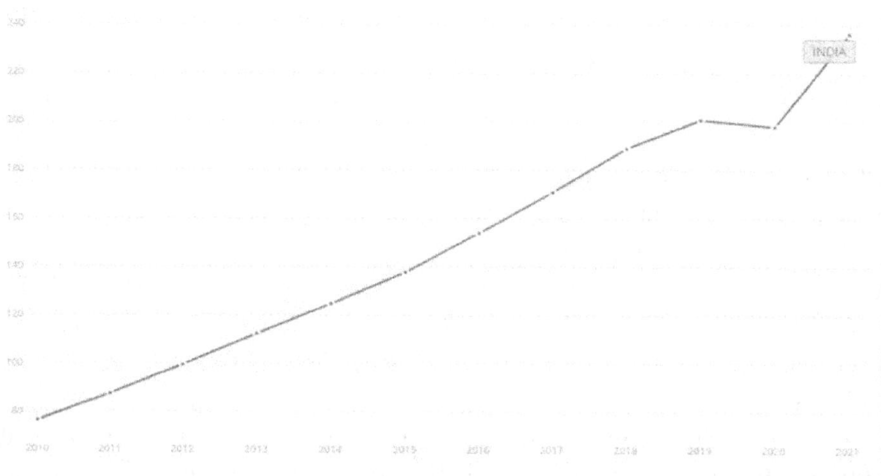

Source: Compiled from World Bank Data (accessed September 2022)

CHAPTER NINE

Important Economic Parameters

Gross Domestic Product (GDP) and Gross National Product(GNP):

The GDP is the benchmark indicator for economic growth in the country. **Gross domestic product (GDP)** refers to the market value of all final goods and services produced within a country in a given period. GDP per capita is often considered an indicator of a country's standard of living.

Gross National Product (GNP) is the market value of all products and services produced in one year by labor and property supplied by the residents of a country. Unlike Gross Domestic Product (GDP), which defines production based on the geographical location of production, GNP allocates production based on ownership.

Table No. 15 - GNP and GDP at Current Market Prices & Per Capita (1999-2010)

GNP & GDP	1999-2000	2000-2001	2001-2002	2002-2003	2003-2004	2004-2005	2005-2006	2006-2007	2007-2008	2008-2009	2009-2010
GNP at current market price (Rs. Bn.)	19366	20796	22610	24414	27472	32198	36664	42604	49659	55497	65123
GDP at current market price (Rs. Bn.)	19520	21024	22811	24581	27655	32422	36925	42937	49864	55826	65503
% change in GDP at Factor Cost	6.4	4.4	5.8	3.8	8.5	7.5	9.5	9.6	9.3	6.8	8
GNP: Per capita (current prices)(rupees)	19347	20409	21782	23141	25603	29567	33150	37972	43637	48092	55660
GDP: Per capita (current prices) (rupees)	19501	20632	21976	23299	25773	29772	33386	38268	43817	48376	55985

(Source: Compiled from various issues of Monthly Review of Indian Economy, CMIE)

As can be seen from Table No. 15 above, the GDP of India has been rising at a phenomenal rate. The GDP which was Rs. 19520 Bn. in the year 1999-2000 rose to Rs. 27472 Bn. in the year 2003-04. In the year 2006-07 it rose to Rs. 42604 Bn. which further rose to Rs. 65503 Bn. in the year 2009-2010. In the year 2009-10, the GDP growth rate was 8 per cent and in the year 2009-10 it was 8.5 per cent. The projected growth rate for GDP at factor cost is expected to be around 8.7 per cent (CMIE, 2011).

Table No. 16 -GNP and GDP at Current Market Prices & Per Capita (1999-2010)

GNP and GDP	2010	2011	2012	2013	2014	2015	2016	2017	2018	2019	2020	2021
GNP at current market price ($ billion)	1505.74	1870.99	1947.12	2021.00	2097.60	2226.42	2439.59	2713.33	2874.65	2874.65	2641.49	3027.51
GDP at current market price (Rs Crore)	1675.62	1823.05	1827.64	1856.72	2039.13	2103.59	2294.80	2651.47	2702.93	2831.55	2667.69	3173.40
GDP: Per capita/US $	1358	1458	1444	1450	1574	1606	1733	1981	1998	2072	1933	2277

(Source: Compiled from various issues of Monthly Review of Indian Economy, CMIE)

The GNP of India has been rising at a phenomenal rate after the year 2010. The GDP which was US $1505 Bn in 2010 rose to US $1870 Bn in 2011 and reached $3027 Bn by the year 2021. Similarly, the GDP rose from US $ 1675 in 2010 to US $ 3173 in 2021. It is heartening to note that even in the COVID years of 2020 and 2021, the GNP and GDP have risen. The per capita GDP which was US $ 1458 in the year 2011 increased to around US $ 1733 in 2017 which was further accentuated to US $ 2277 by the year 2021.

In the year 1999-2000, the percentage change in the GDP at factor cost was 6.4 which increased to 8.5 in the year 2003-04. The years 2005-06 and 2006-07, GDP remained at 9.5 per cent and 9.6 per cent respectively. It was in these years that the total number of mergers and acquisitions in India also saw a phenomenal increase. In fact, the year 2007 was the best year for M&A in India, in terms of volume as well as value of deals. There was a slump in the GDP in the year 2008-09 and this could be attributed to the global depression during these years. A slowdown in the M&A activity was also observed during this year. Hence, it can be said that the change in M&A activity is positively related to change in the GDP.

Chart No. 26 - GDP and GNP at Current Market Price (1999-2010)

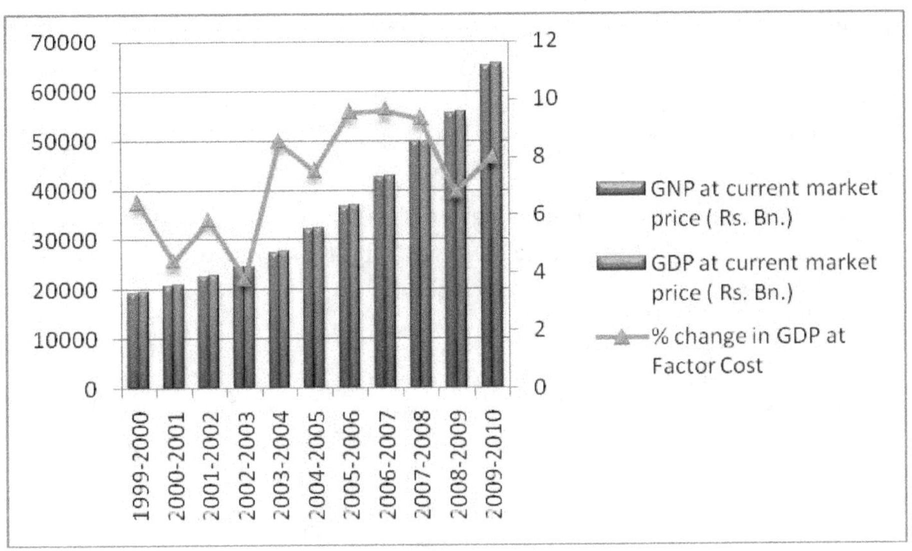

(Source: Compiled from various issues of Monthly Review of Indian Economy, CMIE)

Chart No. 27 - GDP and GNP at Current Market Price (2010-2011)

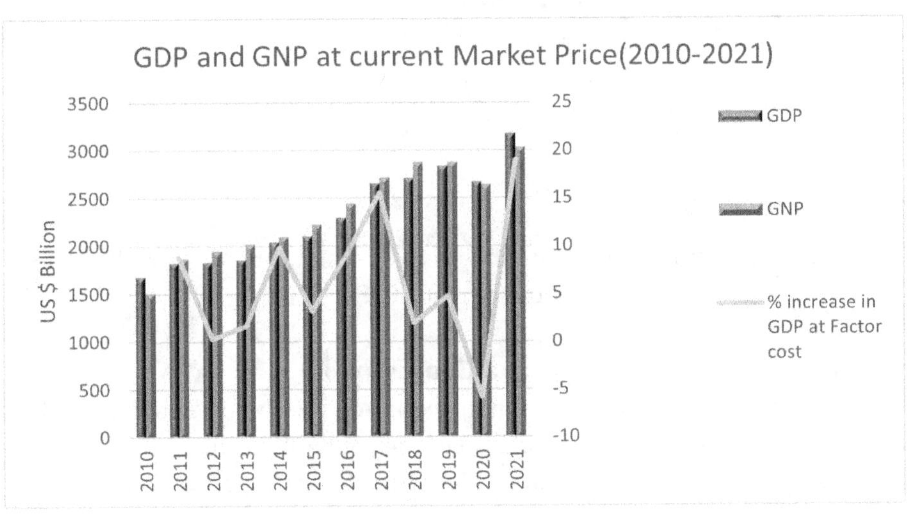

(Source: Compiled from various issues of Monthly Review of Indian Economy, CMIE)

The above chart no. 27 depicts the rise in the Indian GDP and GNP between the years 2010 and 2021. It can be observed that the GDP which was US $ 1506 in 2010 has risen to US $ 3028 in 2021 which is an absolute growth rate of around 101.06 percent.

The year on year growth rate of Indian GDP fell in 2019 and 2020 which could be attributed partly to the Covid 19 Pandemic but recovered in the year 2021. The GNP was found to have a similar trend as the GDP.

Chart No. 28 - Per Capita GNP & GDP at Current market price (1999-2010)

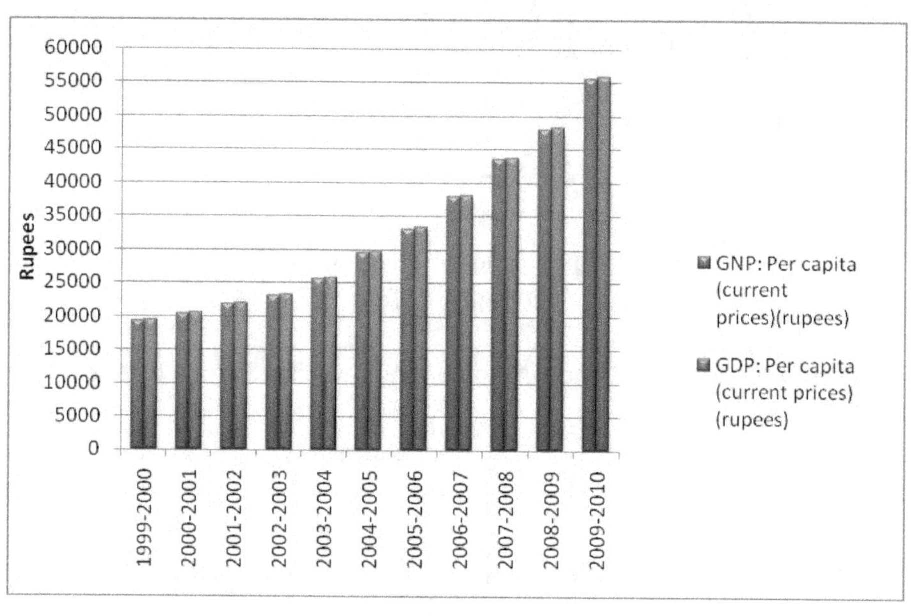

(Source: Compiled from various issues of Monthly Review of Indian Economy, CMIE)

Savings, Capital Formation and Consumption:

Savings form the backbone for investments *viz.*, higher savings lead to higher investments and *vice versa* in accordance with the general perception about the macroeconomic balance in national accounts. An economy can have different forms of savings of which household financial savings generally constitute the largest share in aggregate domestic savings.

Other forms of savings comprise physical savings by households, savings by the private corporate sector and the public sector and foreign savings as measured by the magnitude of the current account balance.

Gross capital formation consists of outlays on additions to the fixed assets of the economy plus net changes in the level of inventories. Fixed assets include land improvements (fences, ditches, drains, and so on); plant, machinery, and equipment purchases; and the construction of roads, railways, and the like, including schools, offices, hospitals, private residential dwellings, and commercial and industrial buildings. Inventories are stocks of goods held by firms to meet temporary or unexpected fluctuations in production or sales, and "work in progress.

(http://data.worldbank.org/indicator/NE.GDI.TOTL.ZS, accessed on 28th July, 2011).

Consumption expenditure is the purchase of goods and services for use by households.

Table No. 17 - Savings, Capital Formation and Consumption

SAVINGS/YEARS	1999-2000	2000-2001	2001-2002	2002-2003	2003-2004	2004-2005	2005-2006	2006-2007	2007-2008	2008-2009	2009-2010
Gross domestic savings (% of GDP)	24.8	23.7	23.5	26.4	29.7	32.4	33.5	34.6	36.9	32.2	33.7
Gross domestic capital formation (% of GDP)	25.9	24.3	22.9	25.2	28	32.5	34.3	35.9	38	35.4	35.8
Consumption expenditure (% of GDP)	77.4	76.7	76.7	74.7	73.2	70.1	69.2	68	67.3	69.4	69.7
Per capita pvt. final cons. exp. (Rupees)	12563	13213	14127	14646	15969	17682	19525	22178	25045	28306	32444

(Source: Compiled from various issues of Monthly Review of Indian Economy, CMIE)

It can be observed from the table no. 17 and the chart no. 29 that the Gross domestic savings as percentage of GDP has increased over a period of time. An increase in gross domestic savings boosts the investment scenario in the economy.

Gross domestic capital formation has also shown and increasing trend over the decade 1999-2010 and it can be seen that GDCF has increased from

25.9 per cent in the year 1999-2000 to around 36 per cent in the year 2010.

As the economy increases its investments in fixed assets, industries would receive a boost which would lead to an increase in production. This would lead to many types of expansion activities by the corporate sector; M&A being one of the many.

As the consumption expenditure of the economy increases, there would be an increased demand for goods and services in the economy leading to increased production by the industries. One of the ways of increasing capacities by the companies is through the M&A route.

Hence, it can be said that a rise in savings, consumption and capital formation could have a positive effect on M&A activity in the country.

Chart No. 29 - Gross Domestic Savings, Gross Domestic Capital Formation, Consumption Expenditure & Per Capita Pvt. Final Consumption Exp (1999-2010)

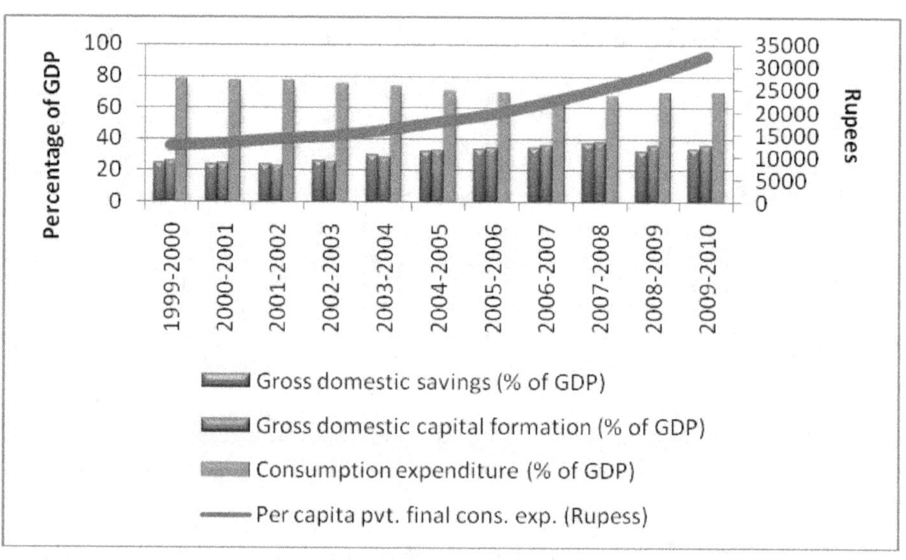

(Source: Compiled from various issues of Monthly Review of Indian Economy, CMIE)

It can be observed from the above chart no. 29 that the Gross domestic savings as percentage of GDP has increased over a period of time. An increase in gross domestic savings boosts the investment scenario in the economy.

Gross domestic capital formation has also shown and increasing trend over the decade 1999-2010 and it can be seen that GDCF has increased from 25.9 per cent in the year 1999-2000 to around 36 per cent in the year 2010.

As the economy increases its investments in fixed assets, industries would receive a boost which would lead to an increase in production. This would lead to many types of expansion activities by the corporate sector; M&A being one of the many.

As the consumption expenditure of the economy increases, there would be an increased demand for goods and services in the economy leading to increased production by the industries. One of the ways of increasing capacities by the companies is through the M&A route.

Hence, it can be said that a rise in savings, consumption and capital formation could have a positive effect on M&A activity in the country.

Chart No. 30 - Gross Domestic Savings, Gross Domestic Capital Formation, Consumption Expenditure & Per Capita Pvt. Final Consumption Exp (2010-2021)

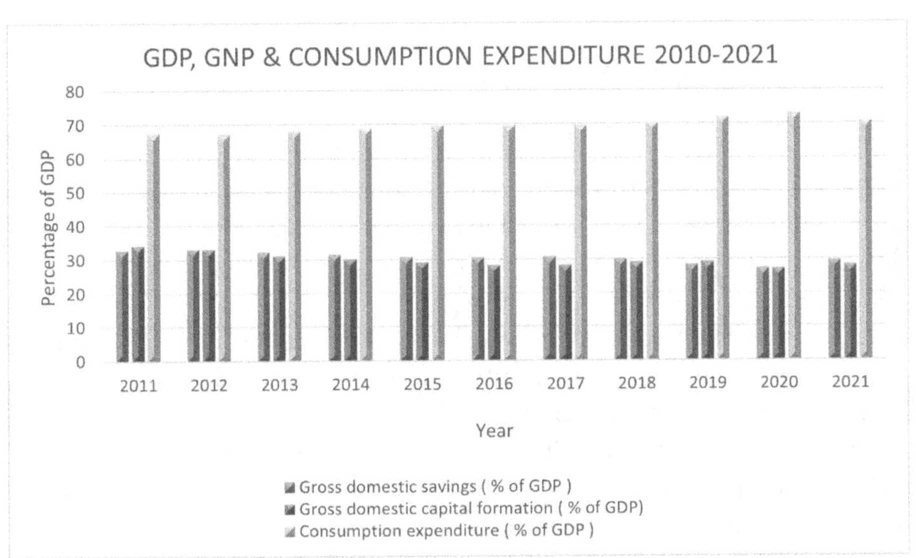

(Source: Compiled from various issues of Monthly Review of Indian Economy, CMIE)

Consumption as a percentage of GDP accounted for less than 70 percent in the year 2011 which has increased to well over 70 percent since the year

2019. Gross domestic savings and gross domestic capital formation for the India is between 25 to 30 percent which is very high as compared to the rest of the world. This is one of the reasons that India is an internally resilient economy.

Exports:

In national accounts, exports consist of transactions in goods and services (sales, barter, gifts or grants) from residents to non-residents.

Table No. 18 - Exports (1999-2011)

External Transactions	1999-00	2000-01	2001-02	2002-03	2003-04	2004-05	2005-06	2006-07	2007-08	2008-09	2009-10	2010-11	2011-12[10]
Exports (US $ million)	36760	44147	43958	52823	63886	83502	103075	126276	162988	183091	178345	245517	297000
Exports as % of GDP	8.2	9.6	9.2	10.4	10.6	11.8	12.6	13.6	13.4	15.4	13.2	14.2	15.4
Percentage Change in Exports	10.7	20.1	-0.4	20.2	20.9	30.7	23.4	22.5	29.1	12.3	-2.6	37.7	21

(Source: Compiled from various issues of Monthly Review of Indian Economy, CMIE)

Increase in exports helps the country gain valuable foreign exchange. As an economy, India lags behind many South East Asian countries and China in terms of exports. However, it can be seen that from the year 1999-2000 there has been a steady increase in exports.

In the year 1999-2000, exports formed 8.2 percentage of GDP which has increased to 14.2 percentage in 2010-11. The years 2004-05 and 2010-11 have been very good for Indian Exports.

The percentage increases in exports in these years were recorded to be 30.7 and 37.7 percentage respectively. Exports provide an option to expand overseas with lesser investment than FDI.

It can be seen that from the year 2011-12 there has been a steady increase in exports. In the year 2011-12 exports formed 24.5 percentage of GDP which has increased to 25.4 percentage in 2013-14. The years 2018-19 and 2021-22 have been very good for Indian Exports. The percentage increases in exports in these years were recorded to be 8.2 and 32.3 percentage respectively. Exports provide an option to expand overseas with lesser investment than FDI.

Table No. 19 - Exports (2011-2021)

External transaction	Exports (US $ Billion)	Exports (% of GDP)	Percentage change in exports
2011	447.38	24.5	19.19
2012	448.4	24.5	0.22
2013	472.18	25.4	5.30
2014	468.35	23	-0.81
2015	416.79	19.8	-11
2016	439.64	19.2	5.48
2017	498.26	18.8	13.33
2018	538.64	19.9	8.10
2019	529.24	18.7	-1.74
2020	499.1	18.7	-5.69
2021	660.5	20.8	32.33

Source: The World Bank's Data Bank

In the years 2020-21 and 2021-22, there was a steep up in exports due to global good conditions.

Chart No. 31 - Exports (1999-2011)

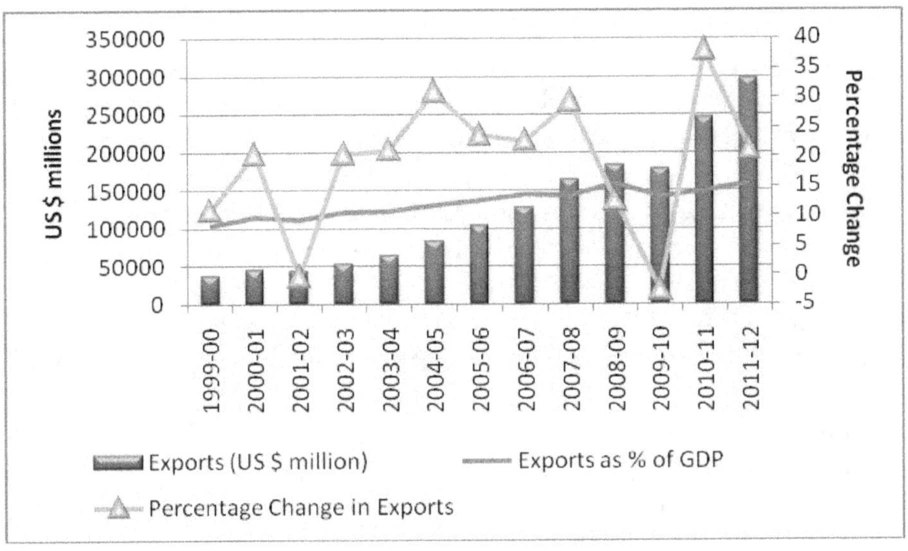

(Source: Compiled from various issues of the Monthly Review of Indian Economy, CMIE)

In the years 2008-09 and 2009-10, there was a steep fall in exports due to global recessionary conditions.

Chart No. 32 - Exports (2011-2021)

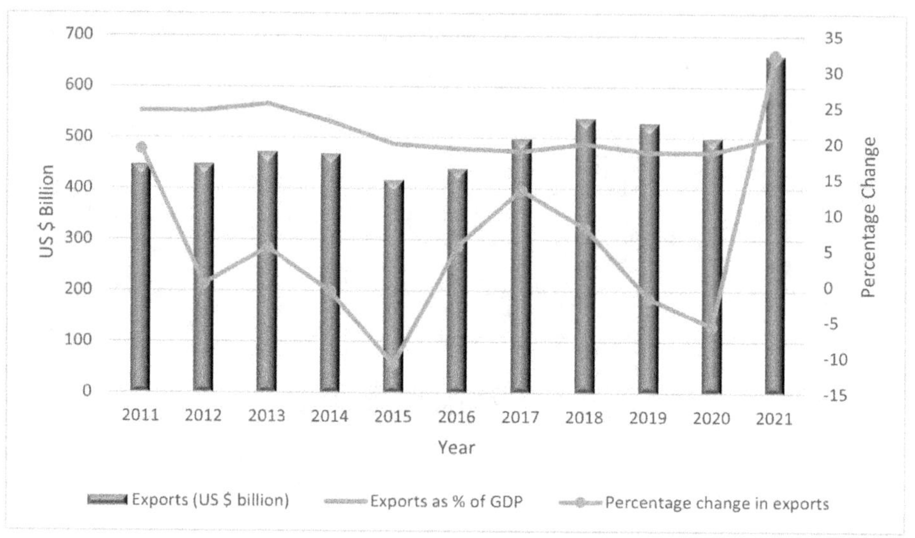

Source: The World Bank's Data Bank

Indian exports were seeing a downward trend since 2011. Bad policy decisions and governance could have been one of the reasons for the same. In the year 2014, a forward looking government came to power and since then Indian exports have seen a steep incresase until the year 2017.

In the year 2020, Indian exports came to a very low point owing to the supply chain disruptions and break in the world economic order owing to the Covid 19 pandemic. However, there was a sharp upward trend in Indian exports in the year 2021 as soon as the pandemic abated. The exports as a percentage of GDP have remained stable througout the period between 2011 and 2021.

Imports:

Indian imports have seen a significant rise over the past decade. As the economy grows and the standard of living improves, so does the demand for good quality imported products and services.

Crude oil forms a very big part of our total imports and India is dependent on the oil producing countries for its crude oil. Imports remain a volatile indicator because of the changes in world oil prices too.

The number of vehicles on Indian roads have also increased manifold which lead to a further increase in imports of crude oil.

Table No. 20 - Imports

External Transactions	1999-00	2000-01	2001-02	2002-03	2003-04	2004-05	2005-06	2006-07	2007-08	2008-09	2009-10	2010-11	2011-12[11]
Imports (US $ million)	49799	50056	51567	61533	78203	111472	149144	185081	249791	299311	287647	350421	427800
Imports as % of GDP	11	10.9	10.7	12.1	13	16.5	18.8	20.1	20.8	25.2	21.7	21.6	22.8
Percentage Change in Imports	17.5	0.5	3	19.3	27.1	42.5	33.8	24.1	35	19.8	-3.9	21.8	22.1

(Source: Compiled from various issues of Monthly Review of Indian Economy, CMIE)

In the year 2011, the imports of the country increased drastically. After that a similar increase can be seen in the year 2017.

This data corresponds to the fall in exports during the same years. In 2021, there was big rise in Indian imports owing to global price rises in crude oil and later on the impending threat of the Russia Ukraine war.

Table No. 21 - Imports (2011-2021)

External Transactions	Imports (US $ Billion)	Imports (% of GDP)	Percentage change in imports
2011	566.67	6.5	25.93
2012	571.31	2.2	0.81
2013	527.56	2.4	-7.65
2014	529.24	3.3	0.31
2015	465.1	2.3	-12.11
2016	480.17	1.9	3.24
2017	582.02	6	21.21
2018	640.3	4.5	10.01
2019	602.31	1.6	-5.93
2020	509.43	-9.3	-15.42
2021	725.55	11	42.42

Source: The World Bank's Databank

Reducing imports will help Indian reduce the current account deficit. But owing to the nature of Indian imports which mainly consists of Crude oil and petroleum, it is extremely difficult for the country to reduce its imports. However, increase in exports and the government's emphasis on

'Make in India' will probably help India reduce its current account deficit.

Chart No. 33 - Imports(1999-2011)

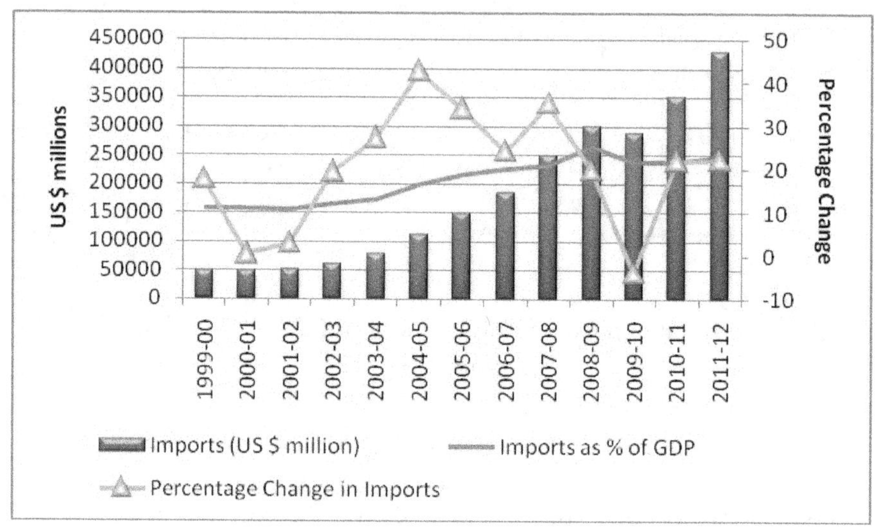

(Source: Compiled from Monthly Review of Indian Economy, CMIE)

Chart No. 34 - Imports (2011-2021)

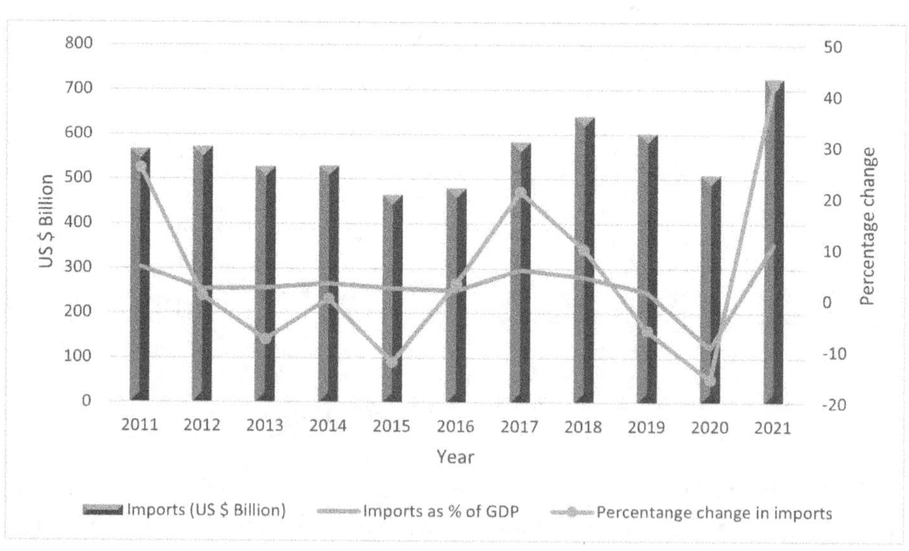

Source: The World Bank's Databank

Balance of Trade:

The balance of trade (or *net exports*, sometimes symbolized as *NX*) is the difference between the monetary value of exports and imports of output in an economy over a certain period. It is the relationship between a nation's imports and exports. A positive balance is known as a trade surplus if it consists of exporting more than is imported; a negative balance is referred to as a trade deficit.

Table No. 22 – Balance of Trade

Year	1999-00	2000-01	2001-02	2002-03	2003-04	2004-05	2005-06	2006-07	2007-08	2008-09	2009-10	2010-11	2011-12
Trade Balance (DGCI&S) (US $ million)	-13039	-5909	-7609	-8710	-14317	-27970	-46069	-58805	-86803	-116220	-109302	-104904	-130800

(Source: Compiled from various issues of Monthly Review of Indian Economy, CMIE)

India's balance of trade has been negative in all the years between 1999 to 2021. This is on account of the fact that India imports more than it exports. However, the problem is a systematic one as India needs to import its crude requirements from other countries of the world. This makes up a huge component of foreign trade.

Table No. 23 - Balance of Trade

Year	Trade Balance (US $ Billion)
2011	-119.28
2012	-122.91
2013	-55.38
2014	-60.89
2015	-48.31
2016	-40.53
2017	-83.76
2018	-101.67
2019	-73.07
2020	-10.34
2021	-65.05

(Source: Compiled from various issues of Monthly Review of Indian Economy, CMIE)

Chart No. 35 - Balance of Trade

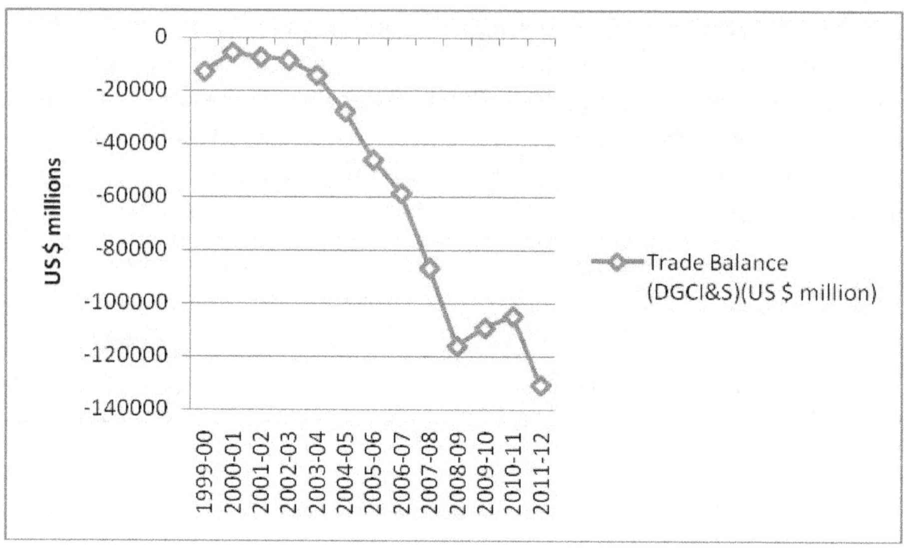

(Source: Compiled from Monthly Review of Indian Economy, CMIE)

Chart No. 36 - Trade Balance (2011-2021)

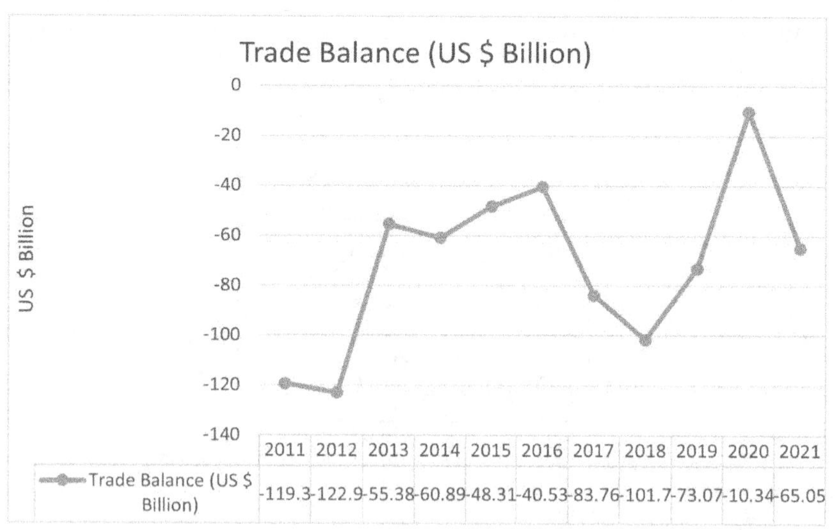

(Source: Compiled from Monthly Review of Indian Economy, CMIE)

India has faced a negative balance of trade situation which has increased at an increasing rate from the year 2002-03. The increasing balance of trade shows the discrepancies between imports and exports. India would fare better by increasing exports as reducing of imports is not a practical solution.

Foreign Capital Inflow(Net):

Net Foreign capital inflow is the difference between all the foreign capital inflows and foreign capital outflows. Net Capital Inflows include Foreign aid, External Commercial Borrowings, NRI deposits, Foreign Direct Investments, Portfolio Investments and others.

Table No. 24 - Foreign Capital Inflow

Year	1999-00	2000-01	2001-02	2002-03	2003-04	2004-05	2005-06	2006-07	2007-08	2008-09	2009-10	2010-11	2011-12[12]
Foreign Capital Inflow (Net)	10184	8814	8551	10840	16736	28022	25470	45203	106585	6768	53397	65748	58583
Foreign Aid	891	410	1117	-3128	-2858	1923	1702	1775	2114	2441	2893	5090	1650
ECB	333	4303	-1585	-1692	-2925	5194	2508	16103	22609	7862	2808	11723	9010
NRI Deposits	1540	2316	2754	2978	3642	-964	2789	4321	179	4290	2924	4049	5450
FDI	2167	4031	6125	5036	4322	5987	8901	22739	34728	37672	33124	12106	11800
Portfolio Investments	3024	2760	2021	979	11356	9311	12494	7004	27270	-13854	32376	32625	28660
Others	2229	-5006	-1881	6667	3199	6571	-2924	-6739	19685	-31643	-20728	155	2013

(Source: Compiled from various issues of Monthly Review of Indian Economy, CMIE)

The foreign capital inflow in India in the decade from 1999 to 2012 has been quite volatile. There was a steady increase in capital flows from the year 2001-02 to the year 2004-05. In the year 2005-06, there was a slight decrease and then again from the year 2006-07 capital flows increased from around US$ 25000 million of the previous year to US$ 45203 million.

The year 2007-08 can be considered as a very good year as the foreign capital inflows increased to more than US $ 106000 million.

The FDI element of Net Capital Inflow is very important as far as M&As are concerned. Foreign companies may buy a stake in Indian companies through the FDI route.

If this stake is substantial, then it can be termed an inbound acquisition. Normally, inbound acquisitions give rise to foreign capital inflow. Foreign companies would be tempted to invest in India if the economy is doing well.

India's net capital inflows have shown a decent rise in all the years except for the year 2008. This can once more be attributed to the global recessionary situation.

<h3 align="center">Table No. 25 - Net Capital Inflows (2011-2021)</h3>

Year	Foreign capital inflow(Net) (US $ Billion)	FDI (US $ Trillion)	Portfolio Investments (US $ Billion)
2011	36.5	2.37	-2.66
2012	24	2.08	-29.29
2013	28.15	2.17	-6.86
2014	34.58	1.93	-37.74
2015	44.01	2.72	-9.49
2016	44.46	2.73	4.73
2017	39.97	2.2	-30.64
2018	42.12	0.936	9.6
2019	50.61	1.51	-24.58
2020	64.36	1.26	-15.11
2021			-5.72

(Source: Compiled from Monthly Review of Indian Economy, CMIE)

The foreign capital inflow in India in the past decade has been quite volatile. There was a steady increase in capital flows from the year 2012-13 to the year 2015-16. In the year 2015-16, there was a slight decrease and then again from the year 2017-18 capital flows increased .

The year 2019-20 can be considered as a very good year as the foreign capital inflows increased to more than US $ 2.43 million.

The FDI element of Net Capital Inflow is very important as far as M&As are concerned. Foreign companies may buy a stake in Indian companies through the FDI route.

If this stake is substantial, then it can be termed an inbound acquisition. Normally, inbound acquisitions give rise to foreign capital inflow. Foreign companies would be tempted to invest in India if the economy is doing well.

The net capital inflows into India was the highest in the year 2007-08. After the financial crisis of 2008, the inflows decreased and portfolio investments became negative. However, the figures recovered in the years after 2009.

Chart No. 37 - Net Capital Inflows (1999-2012)

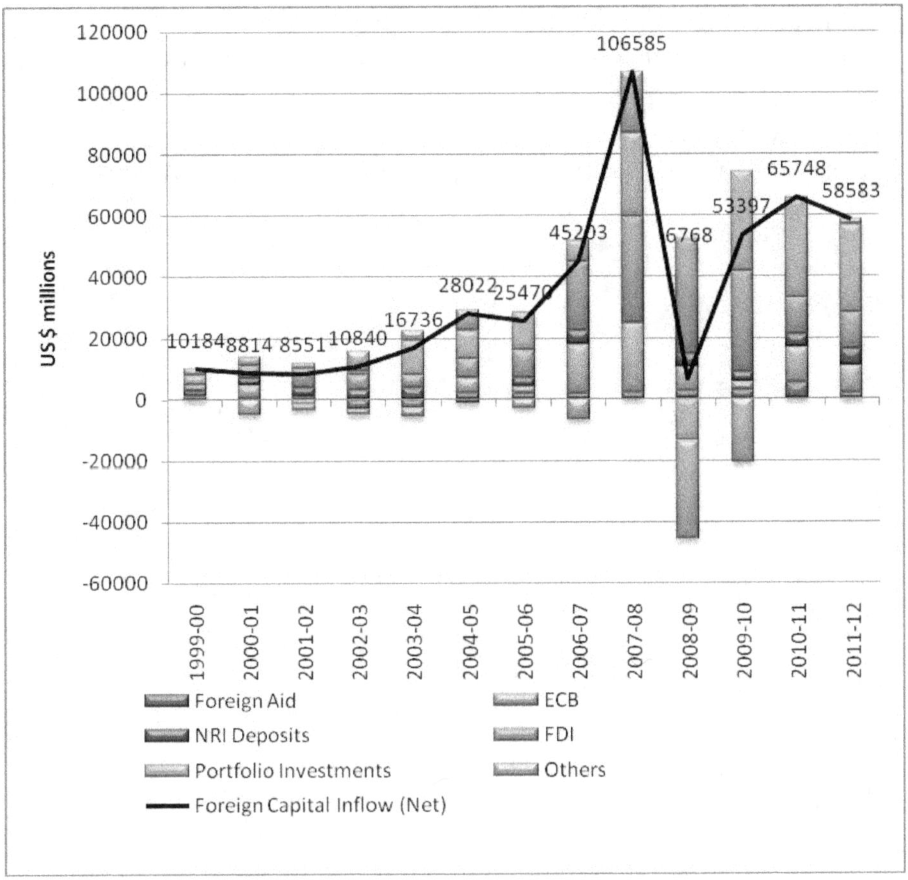

(Source: Compiled from various issues of Monthly Review of Indian Economy, CMIE)

The foreign capital inflow in India in the last decade has been depicted by the chart above. There was a steady increase in capital flows from the year 2012-13 to the year 2015-16. In the year 2015-16, there was a slight decrease and then again from the year 2017-18 capital flows increased . The year 2019-20 can be considered as a very good year as the foreign capital inflows increased to more than US $ 2.43 million.

The FDI element of Net Capital Inflow is very important as far as M&As are concerned. Foreign companies may buy a stake in Indian companies through the FDI route. If this stake is substantial, then it can be termed an inbound acquisition. Normally, inbound acquisitions give rise to foreign capital inflow. Foreign companies would be tempted to invest in India if the economy is doing well.

India's net capital inflows have shown a decent rise in all the years except for the year 2008. This can once more be attributed to the global recessionary factors.

Chart No. 38 - Net Capital Inflows (2011-2021)

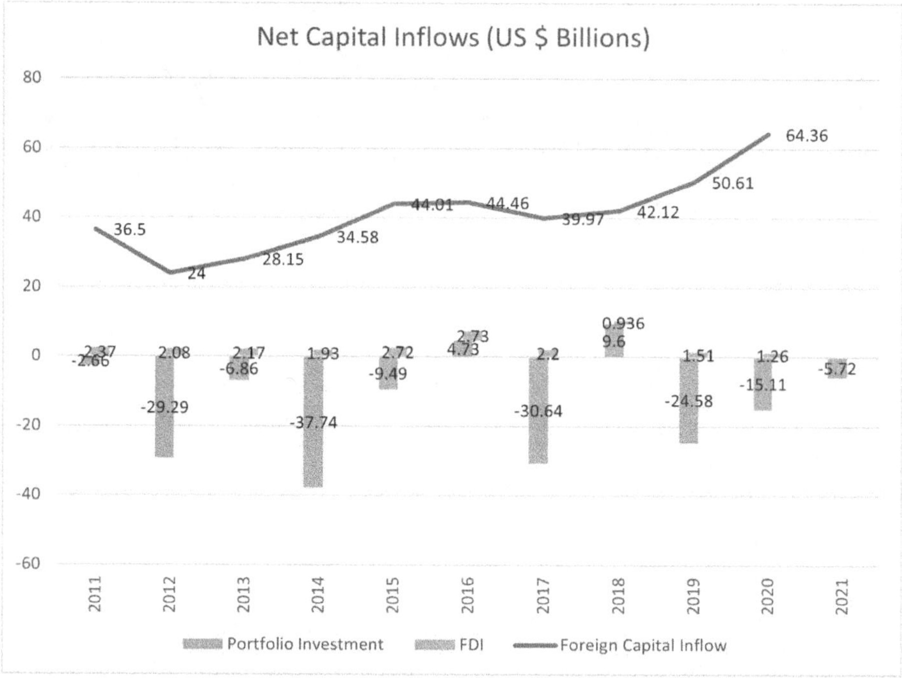

(Source: Compiled from various issues of Monthly Review of Indian Economy, CMIE)

The foreign capital inflow in India in the last decade has been depicted by the chart above. There was a steady increase in capital flows from the year 2012-13 to the year 2015-16. In the year 2015-16, there was a slight decrease and then again from the year 2017-18 capital flows increased . The year 2019-20 can be considered as a very good year as the foreign capital inflows increased to more than US $ 2.43 million.

The FDI element of Net Capital Inflow is very important as far as M&As are concerned. Foreign companies may buy a stake in Indian companies through the FDI route. If this stake is substantial, then it can be termed an inbound acquisition.

Normally, inbound acquisitions give rise to foreign capital inflow. Foreign companies would be tempted to invest in India if the economy is doing well.

India's net capital inflows have shown a decent rise in all the years except for the year 2008. This can once more be attributed to the global recessionary factors.

Table No. 26 - Sector wise FDI Inflows into Industries & Infrastructure

(US $ million)

	1991-2002	2002-07	2007-08	2008-09	2009-10	2010-11 (Apr.-Nov)
Food Products	972.6	392.2	80.7	150.5	348.2	166.0
Fermentation Industries	51.1	216.3	270.1	144.7	112.0	18.0
Textiles	249.2	327.2	186.0	157.4	140.6	56.2
Wood Products	0.1	0.6	0.4	11.3	6.5	0.7
Paper	327.2	139.0	104.2	310.1	85.9	28.1
Leather	43.4	16.8	7.5	3.3	5.1	0.3
Chemicals	1810.4	1934.1	582.3	992.5	611.8	500.6
Rubber, Plastic, & Petroleum Products (including oil exploration)	342.1	464.7	1441.9	497.2	296.2	542.2
Non-metallic Minerals	515.8	877.9	143.0	944.2	45.6	279.1
Metals and Metal Products	223.0	548.7	1176.9	960.9	406.7	960.3
Machinery and Equipments	3092.4	6854.4	2645.7	2528.1	2515.3	1317.1
Transport Equipments	431.1	1130.8	674.8	1151.7	1176.6	533.0
Others Manufacturing	2834.2	1184.7	704.3	1566.1	1079.4	1232.6
Mining (including mining services)	7.8	55.8	458.3	34.4	174.0	75.1
Power*	1885.8	398.5	1011.2	1070.1	1935.2	1028.0
Telecommunications	2140.4	1505.9	1261.5	2558.4	2554.0	1029.8
Total	14,926.0	16,047.6	10,748.5	13,080.8	11,493.0	7831.2

(Source: http://indiabudget.nic.in/es2010-11/estat1.pdf)

The above table shows the sector-wise FDI inflows into the Industries and Infrastructure sectors from 1991 to 2010. The maximum FDI in the year 2010-11 has been in the Machinery and Equipment, Power, and Telecom sectors.

Table no. 27 shows the FDI inflows in the services sector.

Table No. 27 – Sector-wise FDI Inflows into Services

Ranks	Sector	2008-09 (Apr.-Mar.)	2009-10 (Apr.-Mar.)	2010-11 (Apr.-Dec.)	Cumulative Inflows (Apr. 2000-Dec. 2010)	(₹ crore) % age to Total Inflows (In US$ter-ms)
1	Services Sector (financial & non-financial)	28,516 (6,138)	20,776 (4,353)	13,044 (2,853)	1,18,274 (26,454)	21%
2	Computer Software & Hardware	7,329 (1,677)	4,351 (919)	3,054 (670)	47,144 (10,601)	8%
3	Telecommunications (radio paging, cellular mobile, basic telephone services)	11,727 (2,558)	12,338 (2,554)	6,021 (1,327)	46,727 (10,258)	8%
4	Housing & Real Estate	12,621 (2,801)	13,586 (2,844)	4,680 (1,024)	42,049 (9,380)	7%
5	Construction Activities (including roads & highways)	8,792 (2,028)	13,516 (2,862)	4,109 (911)	39,802 (8,964)	7%

(Source: Department of Industrial Policy and Promotion)(Figures in parenthesis are in US $ Millions)

Foreign Exchange Reserves (Excluding Gold and SDRs):

Foreign exchange reserves (also called Forex Reserves) in a strict sense are only the foreign currency deposits and bonds held by the central banks and monetary authorities. Foreign exchange reserves are important indicators of the ability of a country to repay foreign debt and for currency defense, and are used to determine the credit ratings of nations.

Large reserves of foreign currency allow a government to manipulate exchange rates - usually to stabilize the foreign exchange rates to provide a more favorable economic environment. Also, the greater a country's foreign reserves, the better position it is in to defend itself from speculative attacks on the domestic currency.

As per July 2011 reports(Weekly Statistical Supplement- Foreign Exchange Reserves, RBI, Retrieved 20 May 2011), India ranks 7th in the world as far as Foreign Exchange Reserves are concerned. India's Forex position is reasonably comfortable which leads to a good purchasing power parity situation.

The exchange rate of the local currency is positively correlated with the foreign exchange reserves. So, with the increase in forex, the rupee appreciates vis-a-vis the other currencies of the world. In the above chart, it can be observed that in the year 2007-08, when the foreign exchange reserve increased drastically, there was keen appreciation of the Rupee vis a vis the US dollar. However, there are many other factors that influence the currency exchange rate. A good Forex position is an indication of a strong and resilient economy.

Chart No. 39 - Foreign Exchange Reserves (Excl. gold and SDRs)(US $ millions) and the Re/US$ Exchange Rate (1999-2011)

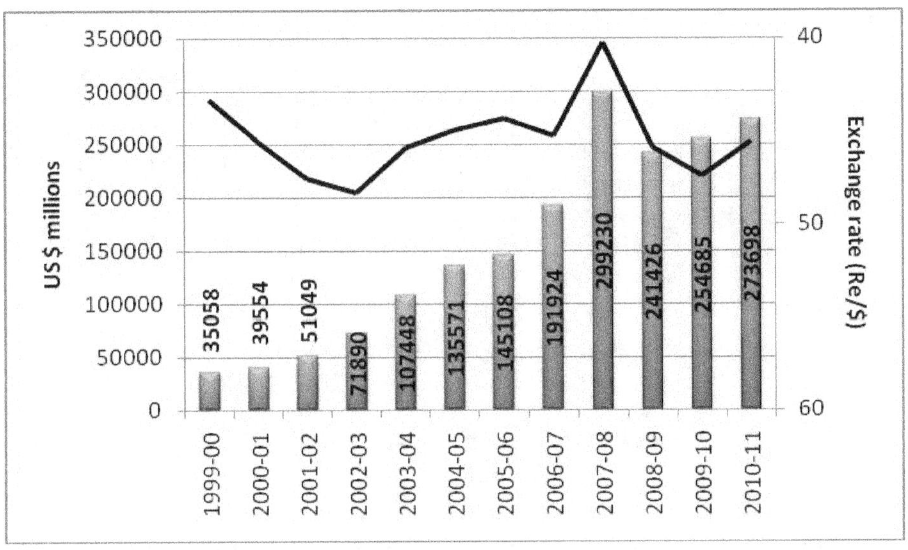

(Source: Compiled from various issues of Monthly Review of Indian Economy, CMIE)

As per July 2012 reports (Weekly Statistical Supplement Foreign Exchange Reserves, RBI, Retrieved 20 May 2012), India ranks 7th in the world as far as Foreign Exchange Reserves are concerned. India's Forex position is reasonably comfortable which leads to a good purchasing power parity Situation. The exchange rate of the local currency is positively correlated with the foreign exchange reserves. Therefore, with the increase in forex, the rupee appreciates vis-a-vis the other currencies of the world. In the above chart, it can be observed that in the year 2021-22, when the foreign exchange reserve increased drastically, there was keen appreciation of the Rupee vis-a-vis the US dollar. However, many other factors influence the currency exchange rate. A good Forex position is an indication of a strong and resilient economy.

Chart No. 40 - Foreign Exchange Reserves (Excl. gold and SDRs)(US $ millions) and the Re/US$ Exchange Rate (2011-2021)

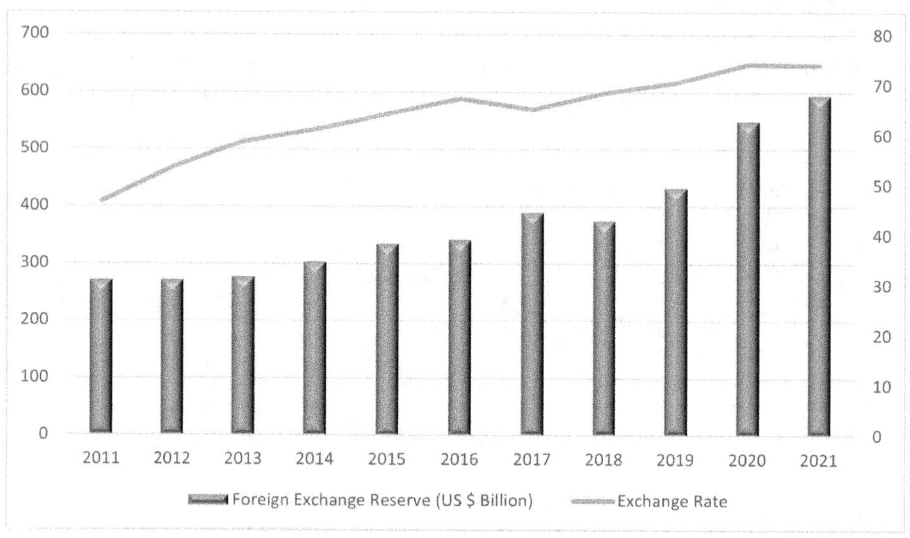

(Source: Compiled from various issues of Monthly Review of Indian Economy, CMIE)

All the important economic parameters were sound and they indicate further growth in all sectors of the economy. A vibrant economy is a pre-requisite for positive M&A activity. Owing to the strength of the Indian economy, the decade from 1999 to 2021 witnessed tremendous cross-border as well as domestic M&A activity in the country. The reflection of the strength of the economy is the Capital Market. A transparent, mature and dynamic capital market has emerged in India during the said decade. There were more than 5000 listed companies in India and the total market capitalization of these companies was close to Rs. 250,000 Billion in the year 2021. Hence, it can be said that the growth-oriented economy of India had presented a lucrative market for M&As in the country.

CHAPTER TEN

The Industrial Sector in India: (1999-2021)

Industries and Services have acted as twin engines propelling overall growth in an economy. They are attracting a large inflow of capital and foreign investments to the country from all over the world. They play a vital role in accelerating the socioeconomic development of a nation, thereby providing several categories of goods and services (both tangible and intangible) and catering to the diverse needs of the masses. These sectors are the largest generators of employment opportunities in the country and facilitators of trade and commerce with other countries.

The industrial sector majorly consisting of heavy and light engineering, steel, automotive, biotechnology, drugs and pharmaceuticals, food processing, mines and minerals, fertilizers, etc. provides immense potential for developing adequate market infrastructure in the economy. These industries are involved in the production of several good quality and skill-intensive products, in bulk quantities and at reasonable prices.

The services sector has always been an attractive investment option for the corporate world. It has facilitated the creation of several infrastructural facilities in the country as well as enhanced the productivity of various industries. It not only helps in the economic upliftment of society but also promotes political and social well-being among the masses.

The service industry comprising information technology (IT), education, health, media, tourism, etc. helps to shape people's opinions about various national and international issues as well as increase their awareness by giving them a participative role in the formulation of policies/ schemes/ programmes/ plans.

In other words, a country cannot achieve a higher growth rate without a larger proportion of services in the gross domestic product (GDP).

The Index of Industrial Production:

The Index of Industrial Production (IIP) is a single representative figure to measure the general level of industrial activity in the economy.

It measures the absolute level and percentage growth of industrial production.

Chart No. 41 - The Index of Industrial Production - Percentage Change (1999-2010)

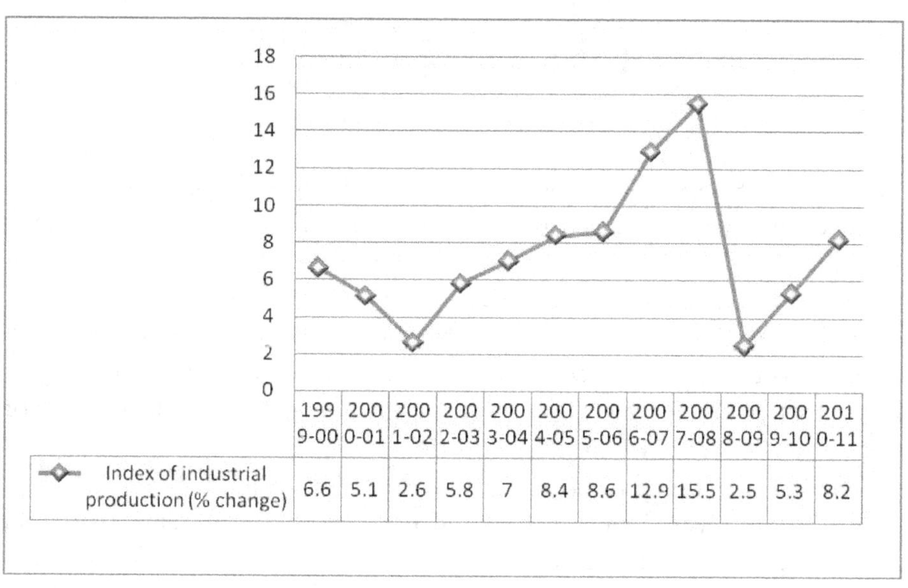

	1999-00	2000-01	2001-02	2002-03	2003-04	2004-05	2005-06	2006-07	2007-08	2008-09	2009-10	2010-11
Index of industrial production (% change)	6.6	5.1	2.6	5.8	7	8.4	8.6	12.9	15.5	2.5	5.3	8.2

(Source: Compiled from various issues of Monthly Review of Indian Economy, CMIE)

The index of industrial growth has been increasing since the year 2001-02 and reached a peak value of 15.5 percent in the year 2007-08. In the year 2008-09, the growth was only 2.5 percent which rose to 5.3 percent in the year 2009-10 and 8.2 percent in the year 2010-11.

Value of Output of the Organized Sector:

In India, the value of the output of the organized sector has increased in every succeeding year since the year 1999-2000. This is a sign that the Indian industrial sector is growing very well and this growth is consistent.

An increase in industrial growth rate and value of output is possible when industries expand their production or new industries are set up. M&As would play a definitive role in the increase of the industrial output.

Chart No. 42 - Value of Output of the Organised Sector

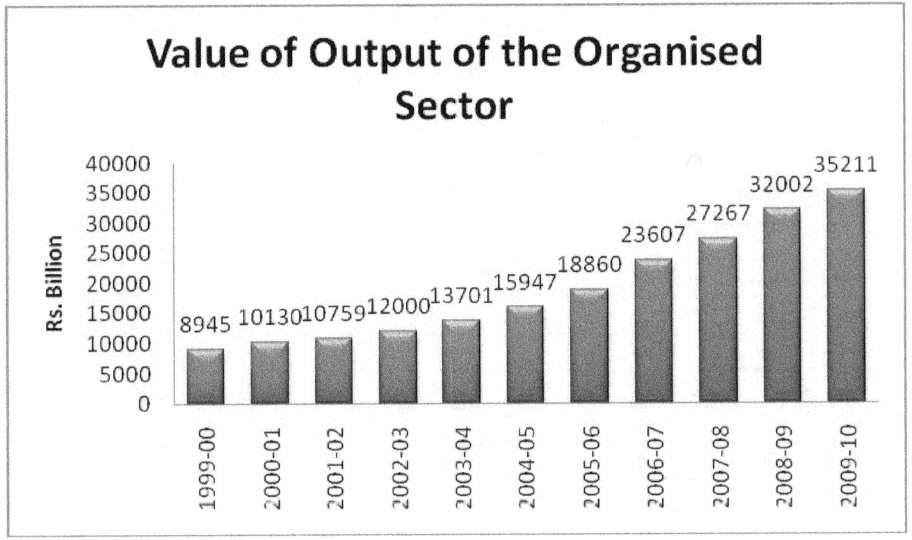

(Source: Compiled from various issues of Monthly Review of Indian Economy, CMIE)

The Manufacturing Sector:

The Manufacturing sector comprises several industries, the major ones being the Automobile industry, the Cement Industry, the Fertilizer Industry, and the Steel Industry.

The **Automobile industry** in India is one of the largest in the world and one of the fastest-growing globally. India manufactures over 17.5 million vehicles (including 2-wheeled and 4-wheeled) and exports about 2.33 million every year. It is the world's second-largest manufacturer of motorcycles, with annual sales exceeding 8.5 million in 2009.

India's passenger car and commercial vehicle manufacturing industry is the seventh largest in the world, with an annual production of more than 3.7 million units in 2010.

In 2009, India emerged as Asia's fourth largest exporter of passenger cars, behind Japan, South Korea, and Thailand.

As of 2010, India is home to 40 million passenger vehicles, and more than 3.7 million automotive vehicles were produced in India in 2010 (an increase of 33.9 percent), making the country the second fastest-growing automobile market in the world.

Table No. 28 – Total Vehicle Production in India (1999-2010)

Year	Car Production	Percentage Change	Commercial	% Change	Total Vehicles Production	Percentage Change
1999	533,149		285,044		818193	
2000	517,957	-2.85	283,403	-0.58	801360	-2.1
2001	654,557	26.37	160,054	-43.52	814611	1.62
2002	703,948	7.55	190,848	19.24	894796	8.96
2003	907,968	28.98	253,555	32.86	1,161,523	22.96
2004	1,178,354	29.78	332,803	31.25	1,511,157	23.13
2005	1,264,000	7.27	362,755	9	1,628,755	7.22
2006	1,473,000	16.53	546,808	50.74	2,019,808	19.36
2007	1,713,479	16.33	540,250	-1.2	2,253,999	10.39
2008	1,846,051	7.74	486,277	-9.99	2,332,328	3.35
2009	2,175,220	17.83	466,330	-4.1	2,641,550	13.25
2010	2,814,584	29.39	722,199	54.86	3,536,783	33.89

(Source: OICA 2009 Statistics. http://oica.net/category/ production-statistics/1998-statistics/)

Table No. 29 - Total Vehicle Production in India (2011-2021)

YEAR	CAR PRODUCTION	PERCENTAGE CHANGE	COMMERCIAL	% CHANGE	TOTAL VEHICAL PRODUCTION	PERCENTAGE CHANGE
2011	3,040,144.00	7.4%	887,267.00	18.60%	3,927,411.00	9.95%
2012	3,296,240.00	7.8%	878,473.00	-1.00%	4,174,713.00	5.92%
2013	3,155,694.00	-4.5%	742,731.00	-18.28%	3,898,425.00	-7.09%
2014	3,162,372.00	0.2%	682,485.00	-8.83%	3,844,857.00	-1.39%
2015	3,378,063.00	6.4%	747,681.00	8.72%	4,125,744.00	6.81%
2016	3,677,605.00	8.1%	811,360.00	7.85%	4,488,965.00	8.09%
2017	3,952,550.00	7.0%	830,346.00	2.29%	4,782,896.00	6.15%
2018	4,064,774.00	2.8%	1,109,871.00	25.19%	5,174,645.00	7.57%
2019	3,623,335.00	-12.2%	892,682.00	-24.33%	4,516,017.00	-14.58%
2020	2,851,268.00	-27.1%	543,178.00	-64.34%	3,394,446.00	-33.04%

(Source: OICA 2009 Statistics. http://oica.net/category/production-statistics)

In the year 2020 India emerged as the 5th largest automobile market in the world. India surpassed Germany in terms of sales. According to *The New York Times*, India's strong engineering base and expertise in the manufacturing of low-cost, fuel-efficient cars has resulted in the expansion of manufacturing facilities of several automobile companies like Hyundai, Nissan, Toyota, Volkswagen, and Maruti Suzuki.In recent years India emerged as a leading center for manufacturing of small cars. In 2011 General Motors; a US automobile company announced to export 50,000 cars manufactured in India and export them.

The Cement Industry: India is the second largest cement producing country with 137 large and 365 mini cement plants. The large plants employ 120,000 people, according to a recent report on the Indian cement industry published by Cement Manufacturers Association (CMA). Cement production in the country is expected to increase to 315-320 million tonne (MT) by end of the year 2011-12 from the current 300 MT. The cement production touched 14.50 MT, while the cement despatches quantity was registered at 14.28 MT during April 2011, as per provisional data released by Cement Manufacturer's Association (CMA).

Some of the growth drivers helping the sector to grow are:

- Abundant availability of iron ore in the country with states such as Orissa, Jharkhand and Chhattisgarh are rich in iron ore reserves. The National Minerals Development Corporation (NMDC) plans to expand its iron ore production capacity from its existing capacity of 30 million tonnes per annum (MTPA) to 50 MTPA by the year 2014–15 through the capacity expansion of current mines as well as by setting up new mines.
- The country has well established facilities for the production of steel.

India is 2nd largest cement producer in the world. Of the total capacity 98% lies with the private sector and remaining with the public sector. The top 20 companies produce the 70% of the cement in India. The demand for the housing segment is expected to grow at 6% per annum' through the PPP model (Public Private Partnership). As a result, the per capita cement consumption in the country is expected to rise from 225 kg in 2018 to 435 kg by 2030.

The Indian Fertilizer industry: The majority of the populace of India lives in rural areas and the foremost occupation in the villages is agriculture.

Developments pertaining to different industries are being made on a massive scale to change the country's economy from an agrarian one to a industrial one. It is extremely important for the fertilizer industry India to have development in terms of technologically advanced manufacturing process and innovative new-age products. The first fertilizer manufacturing unit in India was set up in the year 1906 at Ranipat in Chennai. In the present scenario, there are more than 57 large and 64 medium and small fertilizer production units under the India fertilizer industry. The main products manufactured by the fertilizer industry in India are phosphate based fertilizers, nitrogenous fertilizers, and complex fertilizers. The fertilizer industry in India with its rapid growth is all set to make a long lasting global impression.

Table No. 18 shows the production, consumption and imports of fertilizers between the years 1970 to 2011.

Table No. 30 – Production, Consumption and Imports of Fertilizers (1970-2011)

(Thousand tonnes of nutrients)

	1970-71	1980-81	1990-91	2000-01	2004-05	2005-06	2006-07	2007-08	2008-09	2009-10	2010-11²
1	2	3	4	5	6	7	8	9	10	11	12
A Nitrogenous fertilizers											
Production	830	2164	6993	11004	11338	11354	11578	10900	10870	11900	12175
Imports	477	1510	414	154	411	1365	2689	3677	3844	3447	3448
Consumption	1487	3678	7997	10920	11714	12723	13773	14419	15090	15580	NA
B Phosphatic fertilizers											
Production	229	842	2052	3748	4067	4221	4517	3807	3464	4321	4532
Imports	32	452	1311	396	296	1122	1322	1391	2027	2756	3515
Consumption	462	1214	3221	4215	4624	5204	5543	5515	6506	7274	NA
C Potassic fertilizers											
Imports	120	797	1328	1541	2045	2747	2069	2653	3380	2945	3022
Consumption	228	624	1328	1567	2060	2413	2335	2636	3313	3632	NA
D All fertilizers (NPK)											
Production	1059	3006	9045	14752	15405	15575	16095	14707	14334	16221	16707
Imports	629	2759	2758	2090	2752	5254	6080	7721	10151	9148	9985
Consumption	2177	5516	12546	19702	18398	20340	21651	22570	24909	26486	NA

(Source: Snapshot taken from http://indiabudget.nic.in/survey.asp)

In India, agriculture holds 70% of people are involved in this occupation and developments are being made on a massive scale. In terms of production of fertilizers it increased by 11.40%, India ranks second in terms of fertilizers consumption and 3rd in terms of production. The first fertilizer manufacturing unit in India was set up in the year 1906 at Ranipat in Chennai. In the present scenario, niti.gov.in states that 56 large plants produce nitrogenous, phosphatic, and complex fertilizers, and **72 medium and small fertilizer production units** in the Indian fertilizer industry have single super Phosphate (SSP). The growth of the fertilizer industry is rapid and is all set to make a long-lasting global impression.

Table No. 31 – Production, Consumption and Imports of Fertilizers (2011-2020)

YEAR	2011	2012	2013	2014	2015	2016	2017	2018	2019	2020
A Nitrogenous fertilizers Production	12157	12259	12194	12378	12394	13416	13331	13344	13685	1371
Imports	4493	5240	4801	3920	4766	5068	3385	4701	5191	5633
Consumption	16558	17300	16821	16750	16946	17372	16735	17628	19100	-
B Phosphatic fertilizers Production	4223	4368	3830	3960	4121	4394	4567	4594	4791	4739
Imports	3802	4427	2797	1588	1832	2888	2130	3167	2413	2543
Consumption	8050	7914	6653	5633	6098	6979	6705	6968	7662	-
C Potassic fertilizers Imports	4069	3335	1559	1926	2537	2053	2325	26292	2280	2670
Consumption	3514	2576	2062	2099	2532	2402	2508	2779	2607	-
D All Fertilizers Production	16380	16627	16024	16338	16515	17810	17898	17938	18476	1845
Imports	12364	13002	9157	7434	9135	10009	7840	10497	9884	1084
Consumption	28122	27790	25534	24482	25576	26753	25948	27375	29369	-

(Source: Snapshot taken from http://indiabudget.nic.in/survey.asp)

The Indian Steel industry has witnessed steady growth, on the back of various initiatives taken by the Government of India. The soaring demand from different sectors, such as infrastructure, real estate, and automobiles has put the steel industry in India on the world map. Economic reforms initiated by the government in the year 1991 have assisted in the growth of the steel industry. Prior to the reforms, the steel industry was dominated by the public sector.

However, after the reforms, this sector became open to private investments and foreign investments. The 1991 reforms allowed for no licenses to be required for capacity creation, except for some locations. A lot of new steel plants have been set up in the country due to huge foreign investments and state-of-the-art technology.

Tata Steel was the first steel plant established in the year 1907 in India. Some of the other steel plants in the country include Bhilai Steel Plant at Chattisgarh, Rourkela Steel Plant at Orissa, and Durgapur Steel Plant in West Bengal to name a few.

In the year 2010, India was ranked as the fourth-largest producer of steel by the World Steel Association.

Table No. 32 – Percentage change in the IIP for the Manufacturing Sector (1999-2011)

Year	1999-00	2000-01	2001-02	2002-03	2003-04	2004-05	2005-06	2006-07	2007-08	2008-09	2009-10	2010-11
Manufacturing Sector (% change)	7.2	5.4	2.9	6	7.4	9.1	10.3	15	18.4	2.5	4.8	8.9
Automobiles (% change)	21	-5.7	6.1	8.1	19.9	15.1	10.2	10.4	7.2	2.7	28	30.6
Cement (% change)	15.4	-0.6	9.4	8.7	5.5	8.6	11.2	9.8	8.1	7.8	10.6	4.5
Fertilisers (% change)	4.7	2.5	-1	-0.8	-1.6	8.1	-1.4	6.5	-9.2	-2	13.8	1.4
Finished Steel (% change)	12.1	9.6	8.7	7.9	8.7	8.4	7.4	13.1	11.7	1.9	6.1	8.9

(Source: Compiled from various issues of Monthly Review of Indian Economy, CMIE)

The manufacturing sector in India has shown a robust growth rate over the last decade. In the years 2003-04, 2004-05, and 2005-06 the growth rate was 6 percent, 9.1 percent, and 10.3 percent respectively. It jumped to 15 percent in 2006-07 and further increased to 18.4 percent in 2007-08. These two years have been very important in the industrial as well as economic growth in India. The rate of increase in the IIP for the manufacturing sector for the year 2010-11 has been 8.9 percent which is fairly decent as compared to the previous two years. Tremendous growth can be observed in the Automobile, Steel, and Cement Sectors. The rise in steel and cement production can be attributed to heavy infrastructure development in the country.

The rise in the GDP, as well as the disposable income of the upcoming middle class, has given a boost to the Automobile sector in the last five years from 2005-2010. The increased production can definitely be attributed to the increased demand. Many M&As have taken place in these industries in the last decade which has further propelled the growth of these sectors.

Table No. 33 – Percentage change in the IIP for the Manufacturing Sector (2011-2020)

YEAR	2011	2012	2013	2014	2015	2016	2017	2018	2019	2020
Automobiles(% change)	7.4	7.8	6.6	11.1	8.8	14.3	10	14.5	-11.7	14.5
Cement(% change)	8.5	5.2	5.5	6.4	7.4	8.0	8.3	7.0	6.2	4.2
Fertilizers (% change)	5.5	4.9	4.7	4.9	5.3	4.9	5.1	5.3	4.9	5.5
Finished Steel(% change)	6.6	7.1	7.3	7.4	7.7	8.1	8.4	9.0	9.8	9.4

(Source: Compiled from Monthly Review of Indian Economy, CMIE)

Chart No. 43 - Percentage change in the IIP for the Manufacturing Sector (1999-2011)

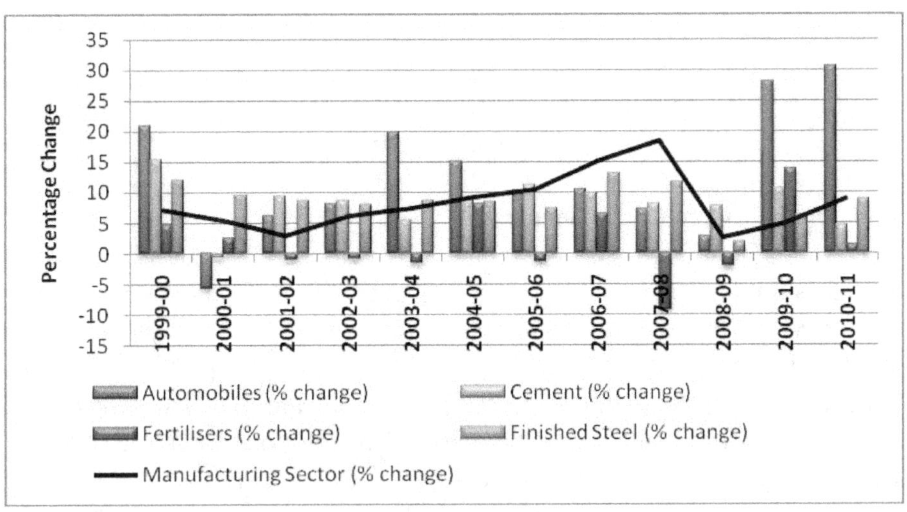

(Source: Compiled from Monthly Review of Indian Economy, CMIE)

The four important industries of the manufacturing sector grew reasonably well during the years 2011 to 2020. The automobile sector grew at a rate of 15.5 percent in 2020 after a bad year in 2019. The cement sector kept up a steady growth rate of around 6 to 8 percent which shows robust infrastructure growth in the country. The rate of growth of fertilizers which was mostly negative the previous decade has shown a phenomenal growth rate of around 5 percent on average. The finished steel sector has seen a robust increase in growth from 6.6 percent in 2011 to 9.4 percent in 2020.

Chart No. 44 - Percentage change in the IIP for the Manufacturing Sector (2011-2020)

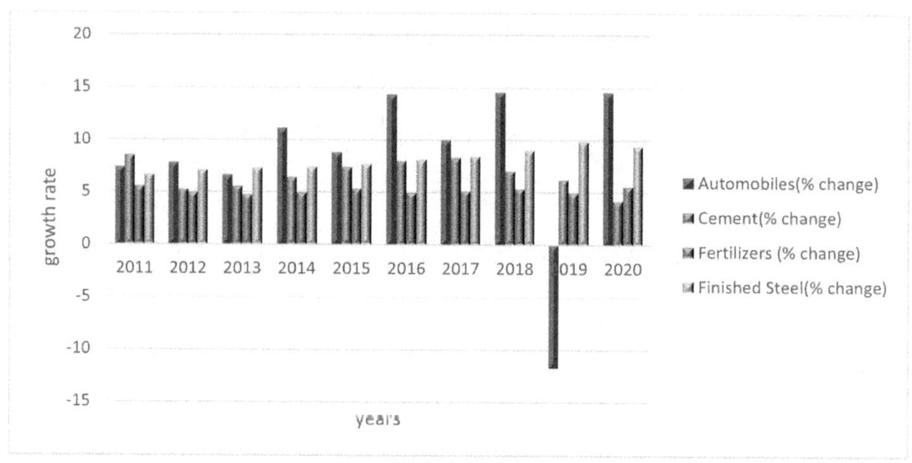

(Source: Compiled from various issues of Monthly Review of Indian Economy, CMIE)

Electricity Generation Sector:

Rapid economic growth has created a growing need for dependable and reliable supplies of electricity, gas and petroleum products. Due to the fast-paced growth of India's economy. the country's energy demand has grown an average of 3.6 percent per annum over the past 30 years. In December 2010, the installed power generation capacity of India stood at 165,000 megawatts and percapita energy consumption stood at 612 KWh. The country's annual energy production increased from about 190 billion kWh in 1986 to more than 680 billion kWh in the year 2006. The total demand for electricity in India is expected to cross 950,000 MW by the year 2030. Four major economic and social drivers characterize the energy policies of India: a rapidly growing economy, increasing household incomes, limited domestic reserves of fossil fuels and the adverse impact on the environment of rapid development in urban and regional areas (Citigroup, 2010).

Chart No. 45 - Percentage change in the IIP for the Electricity Sector (1999-2011)

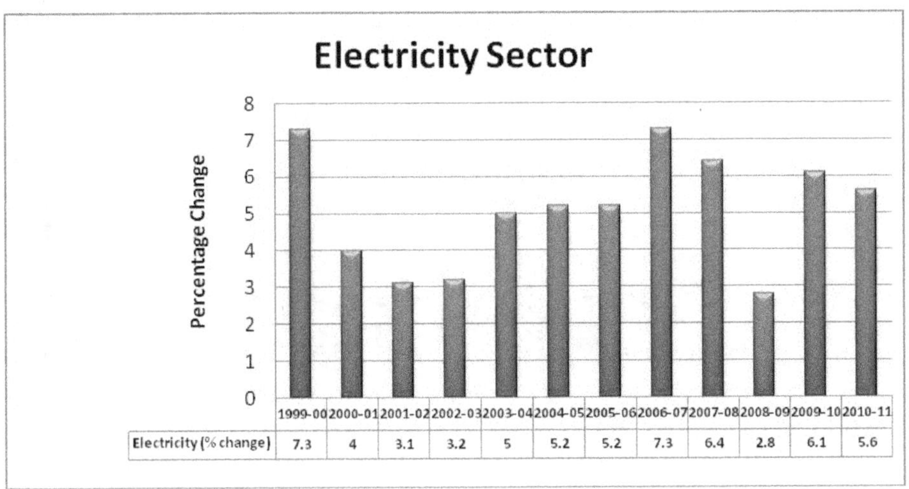

Electricity (% change)	1999-00	2000-01	2001-02	2002-03	2003-04	2004-05	2005-06	2006-07	2007-08	2008-09	2009-10	2010-11
	7.3	4	3.1	3.2	5	5.2	5.2	7.3	6.4	2.8	6.1	5.6

(Source: Compiled from various issues of Monthly Review of Indian Economy, CMIE)

The growth of the electricity sector was 7.3 percent in the year 1999-2000 which declined to 4 percent in the year 2000-01 which further reduced to 3.1 and 3.2 percent in the next two years. In the year 2006-07, the growth rate was 7.3 percent, and 5.6 percent in the year 2010-11. There is a tremendous dearth of electricity in India and hence the future of this industry is very bright. However, government regulation is very high and that is one of the reasons for the slow growth in this sector.

The country's energy demand has grown an average of 4.3 percent per annum over the past 30 years. In June 2022, the installed power generation capacity of India stood at 403.759 GW and per capita energy consumption stood at 1208 Kwh the country's annual energy production increased from about 190 billion kwh in 1986 to more than 1300 billion kwh in the year 2020. the total demand for electricity in India is expected to cross 9,50,000 MW by the year 2030. four major economic and social drivers characterize the energy policies of India: a rapidly growing economy, increasing household incomes, limited domestic reserves of fossil fuels, and the adverse impact on the environment of rapid development in urban and regional areas.

Chart No. 46 - Percentage change in the IIP for the Electricity Sector (2012-2022)

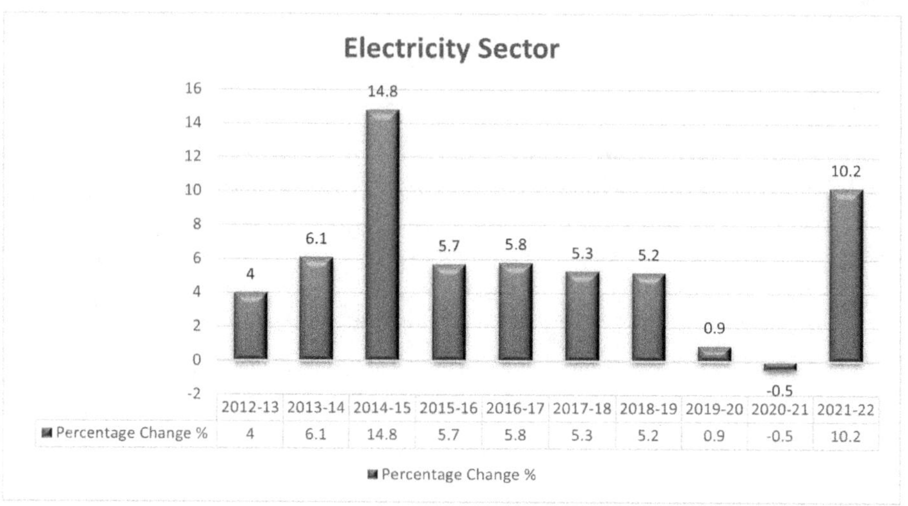

	2012-13	2013-14	2014-15	2015-16	2016-17	2017-18	2018-19	2019-20	2020-21	2021-22
Percentage Change %	4	6.1	14.8	5.7	5.8	5.3	5.2	0.9	-0.5	10.2

(Source: https://pib.gov.in/PressReleasePage.aspx?PRID=1786593)

The growth of the electricity sector was 4.0 percent in the year 2012-13 which increase to 6.1 percent in the year 2013-14 which further increased to 14.8 percent in the next year. in the following year, growth declined to 5.7 percent. in the year 2016-17, the growth rate was 5.8 percent, and 5.3 percent in the year 2017-18 percent. in 2020-21 the growth of electricity is negative due to covid effect and in next year it surged to 10.2 percent. India was a power deficit country before 2014. However, now the electricity generation in India has increased manifold.

Mining and Quarrying Sector:

India is a major mineral producer in Asia and globally. It is currently a global producer of chromite, coal, iron ore, and bauxite. India has been enjoying economic growth during the nineties. Several of India's current state-owned mining and beneficiation companies have been faced with drastic production cuts, resulting in operations becoming uneconomical. This has resulted in the closure of several mining operations. Reasons for poor results have been given as lower grade reserves and excessive manpower quotas.

Since the enunciation of the National Mineral Policy, of the year 1993, India has made good progress in attracting foreign investment in its mining sector, with attractive incentives. The National Mineral Policy was revised in the year 1994 and as a result, private investment (both domestic and foreign), has been permitted for the exploration and exploitation of the following minerals: Iron – ore, Copper, Manganese, Lead, Chrome ore, Zinc, Sulphur, Molybdenum, Gold, Tungsten ore, Diamond, Nickel and Platinum group of metals.

As a result, several foreign companies have begun investing in India, with the majority coming from Canada and the USA, followed by Australia, the UK, and South Africa. Most interest has been shown in the base metals, diamond, mineral sands, and gold sectors.

Chart No. 47 - Percentage change in the IIP for the Mining and Quarrying Sector (1999-2011)

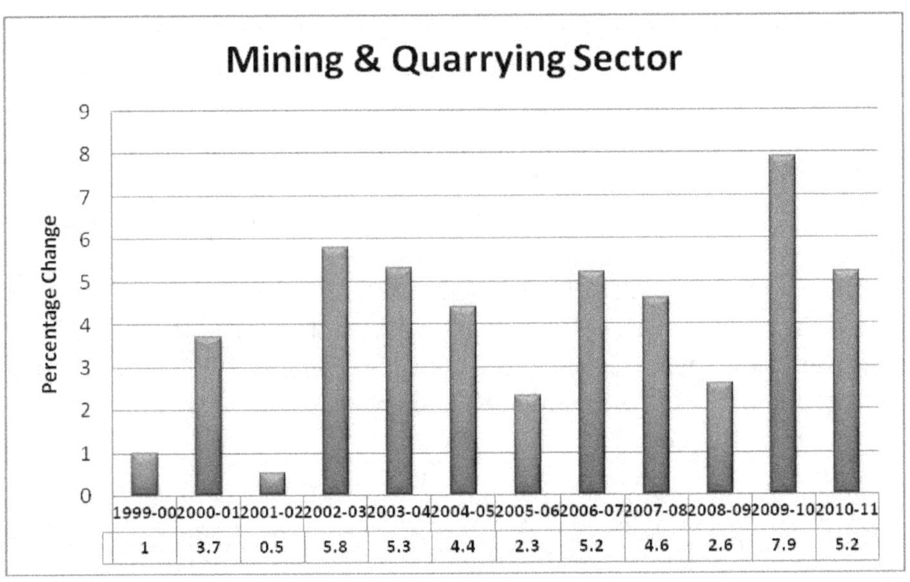

(Source: Compiled from various issues of Monthly Review of Indian Economy, CMIE)

The mining and quarrying sector has shown consistent year-on-year growth in the entire decade from the year 2000 to the year 2010.

However, the mining and quarrying sector has been declining from the year 2010 to 2014. For two consecutive years from 2015 to 2017, the sector saw a good growth rate of around 5 percent. The years post-2017 have seen a steady decline in the sector. This can also be attributed to the government regulation of the sector.

Chart No. 48 - Mining and Quarrying Sector

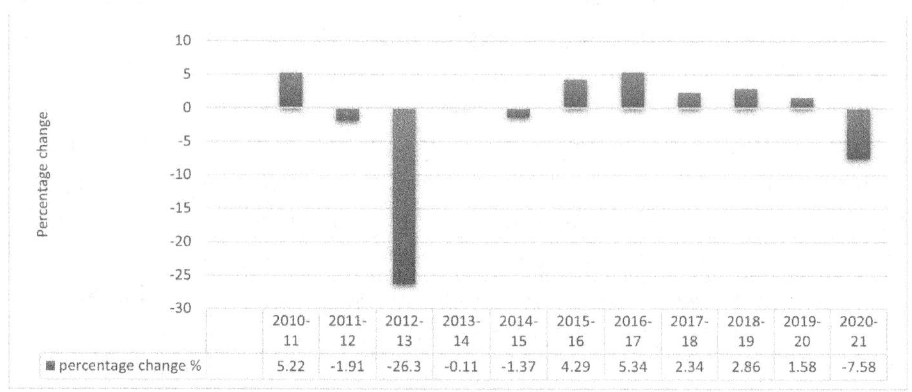

	2010-11	2011-12	2012-13	2013-14	2014-15	2015-16	2016-17	2017-18	2018-19	2019-20	2020-21
■ percentage change %	5.22	-1.91	-26.3	-0.11	-1.37	4.29	5.34	2.34	2.86	1.58	-7.58

(Source: Compiled from various issues of Monthly Review of Indian Economy, CMIE)

The Pharmaceutical Sector:

India's pharmaceutical industry is the third largest in the world in terms of volume and stands 14th in terms of value. The domestic pharma sector continued its strong show in the year 2010 and recorded a 16.5 percent growth from January-December. India will join the league of top 10 global pharmaceuticals markets in terms of sales by the year 2020 with the total value reaching US$ 50 billion by then, according to a report by PricewaterhouseCoopers (PwC). The pharmaceutical industry of India also ranks very high in terms of technology, quality, and range of medicines manufactured. The pharmaceutical industry in India also fulfills around 70 percent of the country's demand for bulk drugs, drug intermediates, pharmaceutical formulations, chemicals, tablets, capsules, orals, and injectibles.

India is one of the fastest-growing pharmaceutical markets in the world, and its market size has nearly doubled since the year 2005. The Indian pharmaceutical market is expected to reach US$ 20 billion by the year 2015, growing at a compound annual growth rate (CAGR) of 11.7 percent during the years 2005–2015 and establish its presence among the world's leading 10 markets. It is the third-largest market in the world in terms of volume and the fourteenth in terms of value.

Chart No. 49 - Market Size of the Indian Pharmaceuticals Industry (2005-2015)

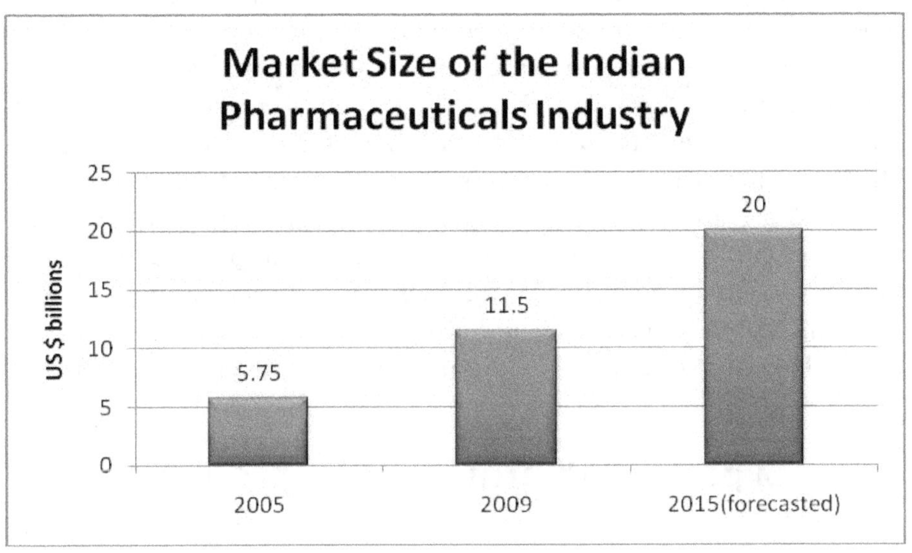

(Sources: Taking wings, Ernst & Young, 2009; The Economic Times, 30 July 2009)

Chart No. 50 - Market Size of the Indian Pharmaceuticals Industry (2013-2030 forecasted)

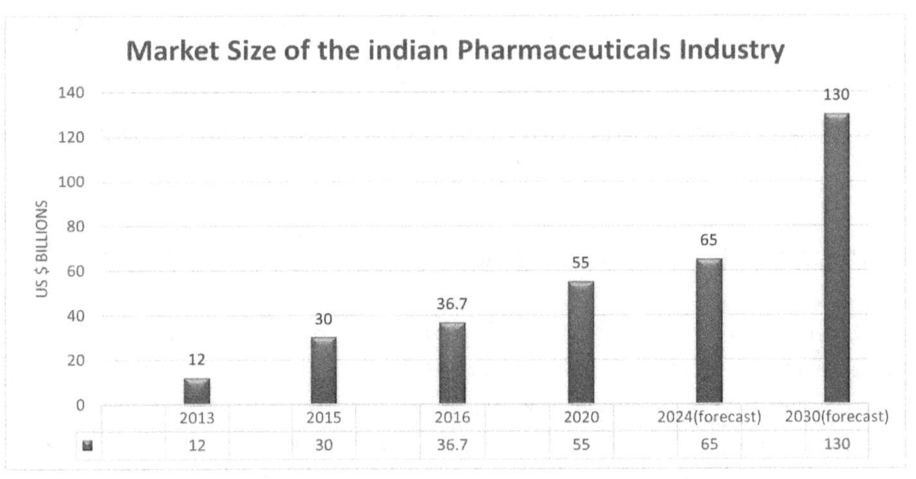

(Source: Ibef.org)

The pharma sector is expected to reach US $ 65 Billions by 2024 and US $ 130 by the year 2030. The sector showed its strength during the Covid 19 pandemic when India successfully manufactured the Covid 19 vaccine with high efficacy and also exported the vaccine to many countries of the world. India is one of the fastest-growing pharmaceutical markets in the world, and its market size has increased nearly four times since the year 2015. The Indian pharmaceutical market is expected to reach US $ 65 billion by the year 2024, growing at a compound annual growth rate (CAGR) of 11.7 percent during the years 2015-2024 and establishing its presence among the world's leading 5 markets. It is the third-largest market in the world in terms of volume and the fourteenth in terms of value.

Chart No. 51 - Exports of Pharmaceutical Products (2003-2010)

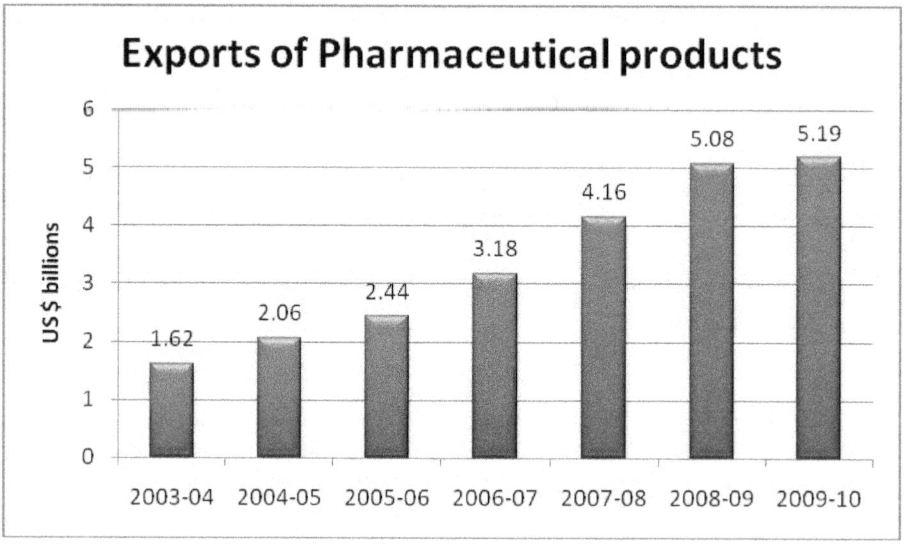

(Source: http://www.ibef.org/download/Pharmaceuticals_270111.pdf)

Exports of pharmaceutical products have more than doubled over three years to around US $ 5.2 billion in the year 2009–2010. The export of drugs, pharmaceuticals, and fine chemicals increased from US$ 7.24 billion in the year 2007–08 to around US$ 9.35 billion in the year 2008–09. This increase can be mainly attributed to increased exports to the African region, driven by funding support from the Pharmaceutical Export Promotion Council for the brand promotion of the Indian pharmaceutical industry in Africa. In addition, the pharmaceutical sector has been included in market-linked focus product schemes.

Chart No. 52 - Exports of Pharmaceutical Products (2010-2021)

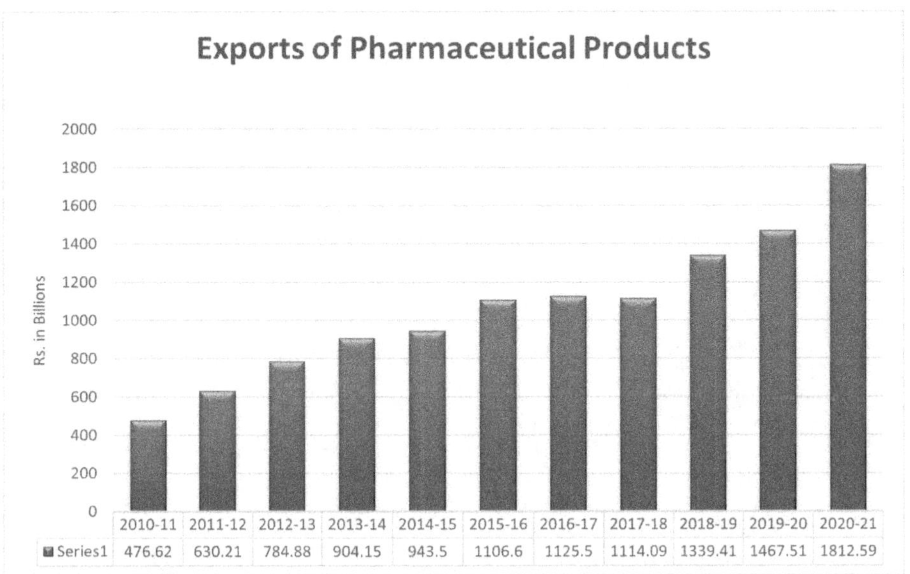

(Source: https://www.statista.com/statistics/624028/export-value-of-drugs-and-pharmaceuticals-india/)

Exports of pharmaceutical products have more than four times over one decade. The export of drugs, pharmaceuticals, and fine chemicals has increased from 1114.09 billion rupees in the year 2017-18 to around 1339.41 billion rupees in the year 2018-19. This increase can be mainly attributed to increased exports to the African region, driven by funding support from the pharmaceutical export promotion council for the brand promotion of the Indian pharmaceutical industry in Africa. In addition, the pharmaceutical sector has been included in market-linked focus product schemes.

Overall production of the core industries, like petroleum refinery products, electricity, cement, and finished steel, etc. has marginally gone up so far during the past few years but there is a huge gap in terms of the required capacity addition needed to catch up with the projected demand in some sectors. There has not been significant capacity addition in some of the core industries. Likewise, the slow rate of capacity addition in physical infrastructure sectors is constricting industrial sector growth. Capacity addition in core sectors and removal of infrastructure bottlenecks would spur industrial sector output in the medium to long term. Capacity addition can be facilitated through outbound M&As and foreign buyouts.

CHAPTER ELEVEN

The Services Sector in India: (1999-2021)

The service industry forms the backbone of the social and economic development of a region. It has emerged as the most significant and fastest-growing sector in the world economy, making higher contributions to global output and employment. Its growth rate has been higher than that of the agriculture and manufacturing sectors.

It is a large and dynamic part of the Indian economy in terms of employment potential and contribution to national income. It covers a wide range of activities, such as trading, transportation and communication, financial, real estate, and business services, as well as community, social, and personal services.

In India, the services sector, as a whole, contributed as much as 68.6 percent of the overall average growth in the gross domestic product (GDP) between the years 2002-03 and 2006-07.

Services play a very important role in the economy. In the year 2009-10, services formed 63.4 percent share of the GDP and this share has been increasing year on year from 2004-05. Trade has the highest share in the GDP out of all the services amounting to 14.9 percent.

The share of Real estate business services is around 11.4 percent. The share of banking and insurance is 5.4 percent.

India has emerged as a strong service provider to the world.

Ranging from communications to transport, finance, education, tourism, the services sector has become the backbone of the global economy and the most dynamic component of international trade.

The services accounts for around 55 per cent of total size of the economy, about 38 per cent of total exports and two-thirds of total FDI inflows into India.

Table No. 34 - Share of Services in GDP Factor Cost (Current Prices)

	2004-05	2005-06	2006-07	2007-08	2008-09@	2009-10*
Trade, hotels & restaurants	16.1	16.7	17.1	17.1	16.9	16.3
Trade	14.6	15.1	15.4	15.4	15.4	14.9
Hotels & restaurants	1.5	1.6	1.7	1.7	1.5	1.4
Transport, storage & communication	8.4	8.2	8.2	8.0	7.8	7.8
Railways	1.0	0.9	0.9	1.0	0.9	1.0
Transport by other means	5.7	5.7	5.7	5.5	5.5	5.2
Storage	0.1	0.1	0.1	0.1	0.1	0.1
Communication	1.7	1.6	1.5	1.4	1.4	1.5
Financing, insurance, real estate & business services	14.7	14.5	14.8	15.1	16.1	16.7
Banking & insurance	5.8	5.4	5.5	5.5	5.7	5.4
Real estate, ownership of dwellings & business services	9.0	9.1	9.3	9.6	10.4	11.4
Community, social & personal services	13.8	13.5	12.8	12.5	13.3	14.4
Public administration & defence	5.9	5.6	5.2	5.1	5.8	6.3
Other services	8.0	7.9	7.6	7.4	7.5	8.1
Construction	7.7	7.9	8.2	8.5	8.5	8.2
Total Services (excluding Construction)	53.0	52.9	52.9	52.7	54.1	55.2
Total Services (including Construction)	60.7	60.8	61.1	61.2	62.6	63.4
Total GDP	100	100	100	100	100	100

(Source: Indian Budget 2010-11)

Table No. 35 – Annual Growth in services GDP (Percentage)

	2005-06	2006-07	2007-08	2008-09*	2009-10**
Trade, Hotels, & Restaurants	12.2	11.0	10.0	5.5	6.7
Trade	11.7	10.7	9.7	6.5	7.2
Hotels & Restaurants	17.5	14.4	13.1	-3.1	2.2
Transport, Storage, & Communications	12.2	12.7	12.9	11.1	15.0
Railways	7.5	11.1	9.8	7.6	9.4
Transport by Other Means	9.3	9.0	8.7	5.2	7.0
Storage	4.7	10.9	3.4	10.5	10.7
Communications	25.5	24.9	26.4	25.8	32.1
Financing, Insurance, Real Estate, & Business Services	12.7	14.0	11.9	12.5	9.2
Banking & Insurance	15.9	20.6	16.7	14.0	11.3
Real Estate, Ownership of Dwellings, & Business Services	10.6	9.5	8.4	11.2	7.5
Community, Social, & Personal Services	7.0	2.9	6.9	12.7	11.8
Public Administration & Defence	4.2	2.0	7.6	20.2	13.0
Other Services	9.1	3.5	6.3	7.4	10.9
Construction	12.8	10.3	10.7	5.4	7.0
Total Services (excluding Construction)	11.0	10.1	10.3	10.1	10.1
Total Services (including Construction)	11.2	10.1	10.4	9.5	9.7
Overall GDP	9.5	9.6	9.3	6.8	8.0

(Source: http://indiabudget.nic.in/es2010-11/echap-10.pdf)

The important services are:

Telecom and Related Services:

The opening of the telecom sector in India has not only led to rapid growth but also helped a great deal towards maximization of consumer benefits as tariffs have been falling across the board as a result of increasing competition, with the telecom service price index falling from 100 in the year 2004-05 to 85.08 in the year 2007-08. The telecom sector has grown from a level of 22.8 million telephone subscribers in the year 1999 to 54.6 million in the year 2003, and further to 764.77 million at the end of November 2010. Wireless telephone connections have contributed to this growth as the number of wireless connections rose from 3.57 million in March 2001 to 729.58 million by the end of November 2010. Tele-density, which was 2.32 percent, increased to 64.34 percent in November 2010. However, there is a wide gap between rural teledensity (30.18 percent in November 2010) and urban teledensity (143.95 percent in November 2010). This shows that the market still has large untapped potential. 10.45 The Internet, which is another growing mode of communication, is a worldwide system of computer networks. Broadband is often called 'highspeed' Internet because it usually has a high rate of data transmission. Broadband subscribers grew from 0.18 million in the year 2005 to 10.71 million at the end of November 2010. The number of Internet and broadband subscribers is expected to increase to 40 million and 20 million, respectively by the year 2010. The introduction of BWA (Broadband Wireless Access) services will enhance the penetration as well as the growth of broadband subscribers (Union Budget and Economic Survey, 2011).

There have been a few very noteworthy M&A deals in the telecom sector, one of them being the merger between Hutch and Essar and then the subsequent sale of Hutch to Vodafone. There is scope for wide-scale consolidation and expansion in this sector and M&A provides the means for that.

IT and IT enabled Services:

India has gained a brand identity as aknowledge economy due to its IT and ITeS sector.The IT-ITeS industry has four major components:IT services, business process outsourcing (BPO),engineering services and R&D, and softwareproducts. The growth in the services sector in Indiahas been led by the IT-ITeS sector which has becomea growth engine for the economy, contributingsubstantially to increases in the GDP, employment,and exports. This sector has improved its contributionto

India's GDP from 4.1 percent in the year 2004-05 to 6.1percent in the year 2009-10 and an estimated 6.4 percent in the year2010-11. The industry has also helped expand tertiaryeducation significantly. The top seven States thataccount for about 90 percent of this sector's exportshave started six to seven times more colleges thanother States.The Indian IT-ITeS industry has registeredrobust growth since the years 2004-05. According toNASSCOM, the year 2010-11 is characterized bybroad-based growth across mature and emergingverticals. The overall Indian IT-ITeS revenue has grownto US$ 63.7 billion in the year 2009-10 and an estimated US$ 76.1 billion in the year 2010-11, translating into a CAGR of22.5 percent from the year 2004-05 to the year 2010-11. The industrygrew by an estimated 19.5 percent in the year 2010-11compared to the moderate growth of 6.2 percent in the year2009-10. Exports dominate the IT & ITeSindustry and constitute about 77 percent oftotal industry revenue. Total IT-ITeS exports havegrown from US$ 17.7 billion in the year 2004-05 to US$ 49.7billion in 2009-10 and an estimated US$ 58.9 billionin the year 2010-11 registering a CAGR of 22.2 percent from the year2004-05 to the year 2010-11.10.52 Though the IT-ITeS sector is export-driven,the domestic market is also significant with revenuegrowth of US $ 14 billion in the year 2009-10 and estimatedrevenue of US$ 17.2 billion in the year 2010-11. The IT andBPO industry (excluding hardware) witnessed a quickrebound in growth and has been estimated to havegrown by 19.5 percent, aggregating revenues of US$76.1 billion in 2010-11 with exports at US$ 58.9 billion accounting for a major portion (Union Budget and Economic Survey, 2011).

Table No. 36 – IT & ITeS Revenues and Exports (US$ billion) (upto 2011)

Year	2009-10	2010-11 (Estimated)	Growth Rate In 2010-11 (%)	CAGR (2005-06 to 2010-11) (%)
Total IT-BPO Services Revenue	63.7	76.1	19.5	22.5
Exports	49.7	58.9	18.5	22.2
Domestic, of which	14.0	17.2	22.8	23.7
(i) IT Services	8.9	10.9	22.5	20.8
(ii) ITeS-BPO	2.2	2.8	27.3	29.3
(iii) Software Products	2.9	3.5	20.7	30.7

(Source: Nasscom)

This sector has improved its contribution to India's GDP from 8.9 percent in the year 2011-12 to 14.9 percent in the consecutive year. The industry has also helped expand tertiary education significantly. The top seven States that account for about 90 percent of this sector's export shave started six to seven times more colleges than other States. According to RBI, the year 2012-13 is characterized by broad-based growth across mature and emerging verticals. The overall Indian IT-ITeS revenue has grown to INR 9921..48 billion in the year 2020-21. The industry's growth has reduced to -9.2 in the year 2020-21 compared to the growth of 20.7 in the year 2012-13. The fall in the year 2020-21 was mainly on account of the Covid 19 pandemic. The total IT-ITeS exports have grown to INR 9921.41 billion in 2020-21.

Table No. 37 – IT & ITeS Revenues and Exports (US$ billion) (2011-2021)

Services Sector Exports (Rs. in Billions)										
	2011-12	2012-13	2013-14	2014-15	2015-16	2016-17	2017-18	2018-19	2019-20	2020-21
(A) Computer Services	1867.1	2447.8(45)	3181.7	3610.8	4104.4	4506.7	4809.90	5580.49	6072.03	6479.08
(i)IT Services	1661..8	2256.7	2936.7	3399.7	3862.8	4300	4572.80	5328.63	5717.12	6146.78
(ii)Software Product Development	205.3	191.1	245	211.1	241.6	206.7	237.10	251.86	354.91	332.30
(B) ITES/BPO Services	617.2	957.4(17.6)	1141.1	1403.2	1658.7	2003.3	2241..30	2661.96	3044..99	3222.33
(i) BPO Services	523	789.6	934.1	1089.2	1336.8	1539	1739.10	2048.14	2361.72	2785.07
(ii) Engineering Services	94.2	167.8	206.9	314	321.9	464..3	502.20	613.82	683.27	657.26
Total Export of Software Services (A+B)	(2484.3) 51.8$	(3405.2) 62.6$	4322.8 71.4$	5014 82	5763.1 88	6510 97.1	7051.20	8242.45	9117.02	9921.41
Annual Growth(in US $ terms)	8.9	20.7	14.1	14.9	7.3	10.3	4.6	11.9	-3. 4	-9.2

(Source: Nasscom)

Financial Service Sector:
The financial services sector in India has witnessed a fundamental transformation since the country was liberalised. India, in the last few years,

has emerged as one of the most rapidly growing economies across the globe.

The financial services market is growing rapidly, and there is significant potential for further growth. The financial services sector includes broking firms, investment services, national banks, private banks, mutual funds, car, and home loans, and the equity market.

Financial Services in India - Key Drivers

- India's high savings rate offers a significant opportunity to put resources into the financial markets. The country has a favourable demographic profile with a large segment of the population under 30 years. The Census 2011 shows that 56.9 percent of India's total population comes in the age group 15-59 years.
- The country will witness a sharp decline in the dependency ratio over the next thirty years – which will be a great dividend. As the dividend begins to pay off, with the working age-group population rising disproportionately over the next two decades, the savings rate is likely to rise further.
- A large, untapped domestic market, with a huge growth potential is available.
- Presence of financial and capital market mechanisms
- A large and continuously growing intellectual capital
- A healthy rate of economic growth

Banking Services

The banking sector has undergone a lot of positive developments in the last decade:

The policymakers, which comprise the Reserve Bank of India (RBI), the Ministry of Finance, and related government and financial sector regulatory entities, have made significant attempts to improve regulation, besides framing policies that are conducive to the growth of the sector.

The banking industry in India is expected to grow by 20 percent a year, with return on equity being more than 18 percent, according to a survey by consulting firm, McKinsey, done for the Indian Banks' Association.

The growth in the sector is specifically being driven by rising aspirations of corporate India, strong regulatory thrust, technological breakthroughs, innovations, rising productivity, and economies of scale.

The sector carries a value creation opportunity of almost Rs 2.5 lakh crore (US$ 56.38 billion) in incremental revenue by the year

2015(McKinsey Research Report, 2010). In the financial year 2010-11, Public Sector Banks (PSBs) recorded a significant credit growth of 22.44 percent.

Net Profits of PSBs have gone up from approximately Rs 39,000 crore (US$ 8.8 billion) to approximately Rs 45,000 crore (US$ 10.15 billion) in the year 2010-11.

The banks achieved 35 percent growth in credit to the Micro, Small, and Medium Enterprises (SMEs) sector against the target of 20 percent.

Nationalised banks accounted for 52.2 percent of the aggregate deposits, with State Bank of India (SBI) and its Associates accounting for 22.1 percent.

The share of new private sector banks, foreign banks, old private sector banks, and regional rural banks in aggregate deposits was 13.3 percent, 4.8 percent, 4.6 percent, and 3.0 percent, respectively, according to RBI's Quarterly Statistics on Deposits and Credit of Scheduled Commercial Banks, December 2010.

Table No. 38 – Sectoral Deployment of Bank Credit

Sl. No.	Sector	Outstanding as on (₹ crore)				% Variation		
		27 Mar. 2009	20 Nov. 2009	26 Mar. 2010	19 Nov. 2010	26 Mar./ 2010 Absolute amount	27 Mar. 2009	19 Nov. 2010 / 20 Nov. 2009
	Gross Bank Credit (1 + 2)	26,47,368	27,56,861	30,88,569	33,71,551	4,41,201	16.7	22.3
1	Food Credit	45,544	40,645	48,562	56,248	3018	6.6	38.4
2	Non-food Gross Bank Credit (a+b+c+d)	26,01,825	27,16,216	30,40,007	33,15,303	4,38,182	16.8	22.1
a.	Priority Sector	932,459	949,287	1,092,179	1,148,808	159,720	17.1	21.0
i.	Agriculture & Allied Activities	338,656	343,070	416,133	411,816	77,477	22.9	20.0
ii.	Micro & Small Enterprises	309,195	335,655	373,530	407,872	64,335	20.8	21.5
iii.	Other Priority Sectors	2,84,608	2,70,562	3,02,516	3,29,120	17,908	6.3	21.6
b.	Industry (micro & small, medium and large)	8,85,393	9,69,261	11,05,051	12,49,843	2,19,656	24.8	28.9
c.	Wholesale (other than food procurement)	67,425	80,922	86,357	94,702	18,932	28.1	Trade 17.0
d.	Other Sectors	7,16,548	7,16,746	7,56,420	8,21,950	39,872	5.6	14.7
	Of Non-food Gross Bank Credit							
1	Housing (including priority-sector housing)	2,79,365	2,91,760	3,00,929	3,27,391	21,564	7.7	12.2
2	Consumer Durables	8187	8028	8294	8928	107	1.3	11.2
3	Commercial Real Estate	92,421	88,581	92,128	1,05,479	(293)	-0.3	19.1
4	Tourism, Hotels, & Restaurants	13,625	15,667	19,410	26,470	5785	42.5	69.0
5	Advances to Individuals against Shares, Bonds, etc.	2287	2347	2863	2935	576	25.2	25.1

(Source: Union Budget and Economic Survey, 2011)

Table above shows that the maximum bank credit goes to the Industrial Sector. It is an indicator of the fast industrial growth of the economy where enormous bank credit is used for expansion, increasing capacity, modernisation, etc.

Concerning gross bank credit, nationalised banks had the highest share of 51.6 percent in total bank credit. They were followed by SBI and its associates at 22.7 percent and new private sector banks at 13.7 percent.

Foreign banks, old private sector banks, and regional rural banks had shares in the total bank credit at 5.1 percent, 4.5 percent, and 2.5 percent, respectively (IBEF, 2011).

India's foreign exchange reserves were US$ 314.6 billion as on July 8, 2011, according to the data in the weekly statistical supplement (WSS) released by RBI.

Indian bank loans increased by 19.9 percent year-on-year (y-o-y) as of July 1, 2011, according to the central bank's WSS. Deposits rose by 18.4 percent from a year earlier.

The capital markets, mutual funds, and insurance sectors have also witnessed tremendous growth in the last 10 years. There is still potential for immense growth in this sector. Major M&A deals have taken place in this sector.

There is scope for large-scale consolidation in this sector and M&As have played and will play a major role in this process.

Credit growth to Primary and Secondary sectors:

Credit growth (y-o-y) to agriculture and allied activities continued to be robust at 10.6 percent in April 2022 (10.7 percent in April 2021). Credit growth to industry accelerated to 8.1 percent in April 2022 from a contraction of 0.4 percent in April 2021.

Size-wise, credit to medium industries registered a growth of 53.5 percent in April 2022 as compared with 44.8 percent last year.

Credit growth to micro and small industries rose to 29.0 percent from 8.7 percent, while credit to large industries recorded a growth of 1.6 percent against a contraction of 3.6 percent during the same period last year.

Credit growth to Services:

Credit growth to services ratio picked up to 11.1 percent in April 2022 as compared with 2.4 percent a year ago, mainly due to 'NBFCs', 'trade', 'tourism, hotels & restaurants, and transport operators.

The personal loans segment continued to perform well, registering acceleration in growth to 14.7 percent in April 2022 from 12.1 percent in April 2021, primarily driven by the 'housing' and 'vehicle loans' segments.

Table No. 39 - Sectoral Deployment of Bank Credit (2011-2016)

Deployment Of Gross Bank Credit By Major Sector						
SECTOR	Outstanding as on (RS. Billion)					
	3/25/2011	3/23/2012	3/22/2013	3/21/2014	3/20/2015	3/18/2016
I. Gross Bank Credit (II + III)	**49,257**	**43713.5**	**49642**	**56572**	**61023**	**66500**
II. Food Credit	**36,674**	**816.1**	**946**	**912**	**994**	**1031**
III. Non-Food Credit	**12,584**	**42897.4**	**48696**	**55660**	**60030**	**65469**
1. Agriculture and Allied Activities	**4,603**	**5225.3**	**5899**	**6694**	**7659**	**8829**
2. Industry	**16,208**	**19659.8**	**22302**	**25229**	**26576**	**27307**
2.1 Micro and Small	2,291	2592.1	2843	3517	3800	3715
2.2 Medium	1,846	2056.4	1247	1274	1245	1148
2.3 Large	12,071	15011.3	18211	20438	21531	22444
3. Services	**9,008**	**10329.3**	**11519**	**13370**	**14131**	**15411**
3.1 Transport Operators	655	728.1	796	895	916	997
3.2 Computer Software	151	154.1	169	176	172	191
3.3 Tourism, Hotels and Restaurants	277	313.2	354	392	370	371
3.4 Shipping	92	88.8	82	99	101	104
3.5 Professional Services	603	638.9	564	707	844	1046
3.6 Trade	1,863	2208.8	2760	3228	3657	3811
3.6.1 Wholesale Trade	1,036	1279.6	1501	1701	1801	1686
3.6.2 Retail Trade	827	929.2	1259	1527	1856	2125
3.7 Commercial Real Estate	1,118	1205.2	1261	1544	1665	1776
3.8 NBFCs	1,756	2218.1	2603	2946	3117	3527
3.9 Other Services	2,494	2774.1	2930	3375	3289	3587
4. Personal Loans	**6,854**	**7683.1**	**8976**	**10367**	**11663**	**13922**
5. Priority Sector	**12,584**	**13992.5**	**15398**	**18781**	**20103**	**22259**
5.1 Agriculture & Allied Activities	4,603	5225.3	5899	6694	7659	8826
5.2 Micro & Small Enterprises	4,550	5190.6	5623	7511	8003	8476
5.2(a) Manufacturing	2,291	2592.1	2843	3852*	3800	3715
5.2(b) Services	2,259	2598.5	2779	3659**	4203	4761
5.3 Housing	2,307	2524.6	2672	3034	3224	3423
5.4 Micro-Credit	268.95	231.1	165	174	177	188
5.5 Education Loans	430.26	482.7	526	579	592	601
5.6 State-Sponsored Orgs. for SC/ST	20.48	28.4	1	2	3	5
5.7 Weaker Sections	2043.32	2563.1	2734	3862	4049	4774
5.8 Export Credit	318.21	377	422	483	426	424

(Source: Union Budget and Economic Survey)

The gross bank credit rose from Rs. 49,250 billion in 2011 to s. 66,500 billion in 2016. Increase in bank credit is an indicator of health for the economy. During these years, food credit was decreased drastically and non-food credit was increased. Credit allocation to agriculture and allied activities almost doubled so was the case for personal loans. During this time, the loan to weaker sections doubled from Rs. 2043 billion to Rs. 4774 billion. The credit to small and micro industries also almost doubled.

Table No. 40 - Sectoral Deployment of Bank Credit (2017-2022)

Deployment Of Gross Bank Credit By Major Sector						
SECTOR	Outstanding as on (RS. Billion)					
	3/31/2017	3/30/2018	3/29/2019	3/27/2020	3/26/2021	3/25/2022
I. Gross Bank Credit (II + III)	71,345	77223	86,748	92631.34	108472.88	118906.38
II. Food Credit	400	338	414.74	515.9	612.54	550.11
III. Non-Food Credit	70,945	76884	86334.19	92115.44	107860.33	118356.28
1. Agriculture and Allied Activities	9,924	10302	11113	11577.95	13340.22	14665.14
2. Industry	26,798	26993	28857.78	29051.51	29623.32	31719.09
2.1 Micro and Small	3,697	3730	3755.05	3818.25	4076.75	4952.81
2.2 Medium	1,048	1037	1063.95	1055.98	1413.39	2422.69
2.3 Large	22,053	22226	24038.78	24177.28	24133.18	24343.59
3. Services	18,022	20505	24156.09	25949.46	27884.63	30361.22
3.1 Transport Operators	1104	1213	1385.24	1444.66	1428.98	1552.2
3.2 Computer Software	179	186	185.35	200.51	196.71	204.97
3.3 Tourism, Hotels and Restaurants	375	365	390.05	459.77	595.19	644.08
3.4 Shipping	84	63	77.48	65.58	77.47	86.03
3.5 Professional Services	1377	1554	1715.17	1770.85	1072	1157.56
3.6 Trade	4,279	4669	5281.58	5523.92	6282	6971.94
3.6.1 Wholesale Trade	1,932	2052	2505.28	2633.97	3185	3417.95
3.6.2 Retail Trade	2347	2618	2776.3	2889.95	3096	3553.99
3.7 Commercial Real Estate	1,856	1858	2022.91	2297.7	2891	2915.8
3.8 NBFCs	3,910	4964	6412.08	8073.83	9553	10542
3.9 Other Services	4,859	5633	6686.23	6112.64	5526	6053.72
4. Personal Loans	16,200	19085	22207.32	25536.52	30016	33748.76
5. Priority Sector	24,356	25532	27390.21	28974.61	41489	45363
5.1 Agriculture & Allied Activities	9,909	10216	11049.88	11466.24	12779.89	13933.13
5.2 Micro & Small Enterprises	9,020	9964	10671.75	11493.94	11865.91	13127.05
5.2(a) Manufacturing	3,697	3730	3755.05	3818.25	2225.91	3047.24
5.2(b) Services	5,322	6234	6916.7	7675.68	4914.95	4935.62
5.3 Housing	3,683	3756	4327.03	4499.45	480.53	450.4
5.4 Micro-Credit	189	264	241.01	382.37	12.44	37.26
5.5 Education Loans	604	607	539.5	519.06	26.66	24.21
5.6 State-Sponsored Orgs. for SC/ST	6	3	3.97	3.88	319.1	306.38
5.7 Weaker Sections	5546	5690	6626.28	7314.09	157.95	373.76
5.8 Export Credit	425	283	155.66	161.14	8705.84	9128.22

(Source: Union Budget and Economic Survey)

The outlook for the services sector which had slightly dimmed due to the fallout of the subprime crisis in the US and the global financial crisis has once again brightened. Recent business performance indicators of different service firms in different sub-sectors also support this healthy prognosis. Even during the crisis year, annual services growth was around the 10 percent mark, which it has maintained since the year 2005-06. This is in contrast to the overall GDP growth which fell to 6.8 percent in the year 2008-09 from 9.3 percent in the year 2007-08. Thus the resilience of the services sector has greatly contributed to the resilience of the economy. It is due to this strength of the services sector that there have been many successful M&As in this sector in the past 20 years. The service sector has an immense potential for growth which can be facilitated through M&A strategies.

CHAPTER TWELVE

Corporate Restructuring, Mergers and Acquisitions: Concepts

Introduction to Corporate Restructuring:

A change in the existing environment of business, calls for a change in the way in which companies within that business environment operate. If the change in environment is drastic, then the change in companies would also have to be as dramatic, sometimes even more so. When this dramatic change is to do with changing the entire structure of the company, it is known as Corporate Restructuring. Any type of restructuring is aimed at either growth or achieving sustainability.

An entrepreneur may grow his business either by internal expansion or external expansion. In the case of internal expansion, a firm grows gradually over time in the normal course of the business, through the acquisition of new assets, replacement of technologically obsolete equipment, and the establishment of new lines of products. But in external expansion, a firm acquires a running business and grows overnight through corporate combinations. These combinations are in the form of mergers, acquisitions, amalgamations, and takeovers and have now become important features of corporate restructuring. They have been playing an important role in the external growth of several leading companies the world over. They have become popular because of the enhanced competition, breaking of trade barriers, free flow of capital across countries, and globalisation of businesses. In the wake of economic reforms, Indian industries have also started restructuring their operations around their core business activities through acquisition and takeovers because of their increasing exposure to competition both domestically and internationally.

Mergers and acquisitions are strategic decisions taken for maximisation of a company's growth by enhancing its production and marketing operations. They are being used in a wide array of fields such as information technology, telecommunications, and business process outsourcing as well as in traditional businesses in order to gain strength, expand the customer base, cut competition, or enter into a new market or product segment.

The need for restructuring:

- Companies may take up some sort of restructuring process in order to **enter new product markets**.
- In **order to expand capacities**, new investments may be made and that would lead to restructuring.
- Corporate restructuring is often taken up in order to **increase the efficiency of the firms**. Efficiency may be management efficiency or financial efficiency.
- Restructuring activities such as mergers, acquisitions, sell-offs, spin-offs, etc. may be taken up in order to increase **economies of scale.**
- Corporate restructuring may lead to less wastage and **optimum utilization of resources.**
- Restructuring activities such as mergers, acquisitions, and Leveraged buyouts in related industries are carried out in order to beat or **reduce competition.**
- Many times, **industrial sickness** may also culminate in restructuring activities.

Types of Restructuring:

Expansion:

Whenever a restructuring activity involves increasing a firm's capacity, market share, product breadth, or any such activity which would lead to an increase in the size of the existing firm, then such a restructuring activity would be termed as expansion.

(a) Mergers & Acquisitions:

Mergers/Acquisitions[1]: Any transaction that forms one economic unit from two or more previous ones is known as a merger.

Mergers are of three forms: Horizontal, Vertical, and Conglomerate.

(b) Tender Offers:

In a **tender offer**, one party, generally, a corporation seeking a controlling interest in another corporation asks the stockholders of the firm it is seeking to control to submit or tender their shares of stock in the firm.

Gaining control is the gist of this type of restructuring.

If one firm wants to gain control over another there are three ways to do it:

- It typically seeks approval for the merger from the other firm's management and BOD.
- **Bear hug**: in this approach, a company mails a letter to the BOD to make a quick decision on the bid. Arcelor – Mittal
- The third alternative is to approach the shareholders of the target company directly and buy shares from them. If approval cannot be obtained from the BOD, the acquiring company can appeal directly to the stockholders by means of the tender offer. This type of forceful acquisition is also known as a hostile takeover.

  If shareholders respond favourably, the acquiring company will gain control and have the power to replace the directors who have not cooperated in the takeover effort.

White knight:

The target firm may seek to join with another firm with which it would rather partner it considers more desirable – a **white knight**.

(c) Joint ventures :

Joint ventures involve the intersection of only a small fraction of the activities of the companies involved and usually for a limited duration of ten to fifteen years or less. Examples: Maruti-Suzuki, Hero-Honda, Mahindra-Nissan.

Sell Offs:

Sell-offs are the opposites of mergers or acquisitions. There are two sides to every deal -The side of the buyer and the side of the seller. There are different types of sell-offs:

(a) Spin-offs:

A spin-off creates a new separate legal entity. Its shares are distributed on a pro-rata basis to existing shareholders of the parent company. Thus, existing shareholders have the same proportion of ownership in the entity as in the original firm. Ex: GE spun off into Great offshore and GE. There is a separation of control. The new entity as a separate decision-making unit may develop policies and strategies different from those of the original parent. In effect, a spin-off represents a form of dividend to the existing shareholders.

i. Split offs:

In a split-off, the shareholders of the existing company get shares in the subsidiary company in exchange of the parent company stock.

ii. Split ups:

The entire firm is broken up in a series of spin-offs, so that parent no longer exists and only the new offspring survive.

(b) Divestitures:

A divestiture involves the sale of a portion of the firm to an outside third party. Cash or equivalent consideration is received by the divested firm. Usually, the buyer is an existing firm. So, no new legal entity results. It simply results in a form of expansion on the part of the buying firm. Example: Sale of IPCL to Reliance; Disinvestments of PSUs by GOI.

Equity carve-outs:

Equity carve-out results when an existing firm sells out a portion of the company via an equity offering to outsiders. New equity shares are sold to outsiders, which gives them ownership of a portion of the previously existing firm. A new legal entity is created.

Corporate Control:

(a) Premium Buybacks:

A premium buyback happens when the company repurchases a substantial stockholder's ownership interest at a premium above the market price. Example: DSP-Meryll Lynch: Meryll Lynch bought over Hemendra Kothari's share from the above company. It is also called *green mail.*

(b) Standstill Agreements:

Often, in connection to premium buybacks, standstill agreements are written. A Standstill Agreement represents a voluntary contract in which the stockholder who is bought over agrees not to make further attempts to take over the company in the future. When a standstill agreement is made without a buyback, the substantial stockholder simply agrees not to increase his or her ownership which presumably would put him in a controlling position.

(c) Anti-takeover Amendments:

These are changes in the corporate bylaws to make an acquisition of the company more difficult or more expensive.

These include:

- Supermajority voting provisions requiring a high percentage of stockholders to approve a merger.
- Staggered terms for directors which can delay change of control for a number of years.
- Golden parachutes which award large termination payments to existing management if control of the firm is changed and management is terminated.

(d) Proxy Contests:

In a proxy contest, an outside group seeks to obtain representation on the firm's Board of Directors. The outsiders are referred to as "dissidents" or "insurgents". They seek to reduce the control of the "incumbents" or existing Board of Directors.

Changes In Ownership Structure:

(a) Exchange Offers:

Exchange offers involve the exchange of debt or preferred stock for common stock or vice versa. Exchanging debt for common stock increases leverage; exchanging common stock for debt decreases leverage.

(b) Share Repurchases:

In a share repurchase, a corporation buys back some fraction of its outstanding shares of common stock. Tender offers may be made for share repurchase.

(c) Going Private:

In this type of transaction, the entire equity interest in a previously public corporation is purchased by a small group of investors. The firm is no longer subject to the regulations of the SEBI, whose purpose is to protect public investors. When such a transaction is initiated by the incumbent management itself, it is called Management Buy-out. Example of management Buy-out: UB group chairman Mr. Vijay Mallya exited the Sorghum beer business in South Africa. The group company UB Holdings offloaded United National Breweries (UNB), the sorghum beer company, to a management buyout led by its chief executive officer and managing director Rajan Ranganathan. The deal size was roughly $16 million.

(d) Leveraged Buy-outs:

Whenever a buyer company borrows funds from third-party investors in the form of debt, in order to buy out another company, then such a transaction becomes a leveraged buy-out.

[1] In many theoretical expositions, the terms mergers and acquisitions have been used interchangeably.

CHAPTER THIRTEEN

Mergers and Acquisitions: Definitive aspects

Mergers or Amalgamations :

A merger is a combination of two or more businesses into one business. Laws in India use the term 'amalgamation' for a merger. The Income Tax Act, 1961 [Section 2 (1A)] defines amalgamation as the merger of one or more companies with another or the merger of two or more companies to form a new company, in such a way that all assets and liabilities of the amalgamating companies become assets and liabilities of the amalgamated company and shareholders not less than nine-tenths in value of the shares in the amalgamating company or companies become shareholders of the amalgamated company.

Thus, mergers or amalgamations may take two forms:-

(a) Merger through Absorption:

An absorption is a combination of two or more companies into an 'existing company'. All companies except one lose their identity in such a merger. For example, the absorption of Tata Fertilisers Ltd (TFL) by Tata Chemicals Ltd. (TCL). TCL, an acquiring company (a buyer), survived after the merger while TFL, an acquired company (a seller), ceased to exist. TFL transferred its assets, liabilities, and shares to TCL.

(b) Merger through Consolidation:

A consolidation is a combination of two or more companies into a 'new company'. In this form of merger, all companies are legally dissolved and a new entity is created. Here, the acquired company transfers its assets, liabilities, and shares to the acquiring company for cash or exchange of shares. For example, a merger of Hindustan Computers Ltd, Hindustan Instruments Ltd, Indian Software Company Ltd., and Indian Reprographics Ltd into an entirely new company called HCL Ltd.

A fundamental characteristic of a merger (either through absorption or consolidation) is that the acquiring company (existing or new) takes over the ownership of other companies and combines their operations with its own operations.

Besides, there are three major types of mergers :

(i) Horizontal merger:

A horizontal merger is a combination of two or more firms in the same area of business. For example, combining of two book publishers or two luggage manufacturing companies to gain a dominant market share.

(ii) Vertical merger:

It is a combination of two or more firms involved in different stages of production or distribution of the same product. For example, joining of a TV manufacturing(assembling) company and a TV marketing company or joining of a spinning company and a weaving company. A vertical merger may take the form of a forward or backward merger. When a company combines with the supplier of material, it is called a backward merger and when it combines with the customer, it is known as a forward merger.

(iii) Conglomerate merger:

It is a combination of firms engaged in unrelated lines of business activity. For example, merging of different businesses like manufacturing of cement products, fertilizer products, electronic products, insurance investment and advertising agencies. L&T and Voltas Ltd. are examples of such mergers. Conglomerate Mergers can be of three types:

- *Product extension:* Broaden the product line of the firm.
- *Market extension:* Broadens the market of the firm.
- *Pure conglomerate:* Merging companies have no relation to each other's business.

Types of Conglomerate Mergers:
Financial Conglomerate:

- Financial conglomerates provide a flow of funds to each segment of their operations, exercise control and are the ultimate financial risk takers.
- They undertake strategic planning but do not participate in operating decisions.

Main Functions:

1. It improves risk-return ratio through diversification.
2. It avoids 'gambling ruin' (an adverse run of losses which might cause bankruptcy.)
3. Establishing programmes of financial planning and control which leads to improved quality of general and functional management, more efficient operations and better resource allocation.
4. If management does not perform effectively but the productivity of assets in the market is favorable, the management is changed. Assets are placed under more efficient managements hence improved resource allocation.
5. Distinction is made between performance based on potential superiority of product or market Vs. results related to better managerial performance.

Management Conglomerate:

- They not only assume financial responsibility and control but also play a role in operating decisions and provide staff expertise and staff services to the operating entities.
- Since managerial functions of POSDCORB are transferable to any company, such conglomerates increase potential for improving performance.

Main Functions:

1. Provides the basis for the most general theory of mergers.
2. Synergy

Economic Rationale for different types of mergers:
Horizontal Mergers:

1. Achieving economies of scale
2. Expansion

However horizontal mergers are not encouraged by the government as they increase monopoly power by the large merged firms.
Vertical Mergers:

1. Technological economies
2. Transportation costs
3. Cost cutting
4. Proper inventory management
5. Removing uncertainty of input prices
6. Reducing transfer pricing.

Conglomerate Mergers:

1. Conglomerate firm controls a range of activities like research, applied engineering, production, mktg etc.
2. Diversification is achieved by external acquisitions and mergers and not by internal growth.

Organisational Learning and Organisational Capital:

- Organization learning: It is defined as improvement in the skills and abilities of individual employees through learning by experience within the firm.

1. Production Knowledge: One case of learning is in the area of entrepreneurial or managerial ability to organize and maintain complex production processes economically. This is called production knowledge.
2. Three forms of Organisational Learning:

   - Raw Managerial experience: It refers to the capabilities developed in generic management functions of planning, organizing, directing, controlling and so on as well as in financial planning and control.
   - Industry Specific managerial experience: It refers to the development of capabilities in specific management functions related to the characteristics of production and marketing in particular industries.
   - Non managerial labour input: It refers to the level of skills of the production workers that will improve over time through learning by experience.

- Organization capital: It is accumulated through experience within the organization called the firm.

1. <u>Employee Embodied Information</u>: It is the firm specific information embodied in every employee. This type of information is obtained when the employee becomes familiar with the firm's production arrangements, management and control systems, other employees' skills, knowledge and job duties
2. <u>Team Effects:</u>

- The role of information here is to allow the firm to organize efficient managerial and production teams within the firm.
- <u>Match between workers and tasks:</u> Information on employee characteristics and matching the job to these characteristics.
- <u>Matching workers with workers:</u>These 3 types of information cannot be passed on from firm to firm through transfer of labour.

Acquisitions and Takeovers:

An acquisition may be defined as an act of acquiring effective control by one company over assets or management of another company without any combination of companies. Thus, in an acquisition, two or more companies may remain independent, separate legal entities, but there may be a change in control of the companies. When an acquisition is 'forced' or 'unwilling', it is called a takeover. In an unwilling acquisition, the management of the 'target' company would oppose a move of being taken over. But, when managements of acquiring and target companies mutually and willingly agree to the takeover, it is called an acquisition or friendly takeover.

Under the Monopolies and Restrictive Practices Act, a takeover meant the acquisition of not less than 25 percent of the voting power in a company. While in the Companies Act (Section 372), a company's investment in the shares of another company in excess of 10 percent of the subscribed capital can result in takeovers. An acquisition or takeover does not necessarily entail full legal control. A company can also have effective control over another company by holding minority ownership.

CHAPTER FOURTEEN

Theories of Mergers and Acquisitions

1. Efficiency theories:

The efficiency theories hold that mergers and other forms of asset redeployment have potential social benefits. They involve improving the performance of incumbent management. Most of the efficiency theories are used for conglomerate mergers.

(a) Differential managerial efficiency:

This theory states that if the management of firm A is better than the management of firm B, and firm A takes over firm B, then the management of B will rise up to the level of A. Social as well as private gain would arise from such a scenario. The problem is that if all firms take up this route, then there will be only one firm in the economy.

It will benefit:

1. If firm A (acquiring firm) has excess managerial capacity and firm B (acquired firm) has non-managerial organizational capital.

2. Firms with below-average efficiency.

3. Firms operating in similar kinds of business activities that are weak in management.

(b) Inefficient management:

This theory is similar to differential efficiency. However, horizontal mergers are more relevant in differential management whereas, even conglomerate mergers are relevant in inefficient management.

(c) Operating synergy:

Operating synergy may be achieved in horizontal, vertical, and even conglomerate mergers. The theory based on operating synergy assumes that economies of scale do exist in the industry and that prior to the merger; the firms are operating at levels of activity that fall short of achieving the potential for economies of scale. Economies of scale arise because of invisibilities, such as people, equipment and overhead, which provide increasing returns if spread over a large number of units of output. This theory says that operating synergies in terms of manufacturing facilities, plant, research and development, management functions, etc. originate due to mergers, and hence gains result from merger activity.

(d) Pure diversification:

Diversification gives an opportunity to employees to improvise their skills and learn new skills and helps the businessman to reduce his risk. When a firm is liquidated, all firm-related information is lost. If a firm is diversified then this firm-specific information can be transferred to the new firm. The reputational capital of the firm can also be used. Diversification can increase the corporate debt capacity of the firm and decrease the present value of future tax liability.

(e) Financial synergy:

Another school of thought says that only operating synergy is not enough. Hence comes the concept of financial synergy. Synergy, with respect to raising funds, internal and external capital, working capital (vertical mergers), etc. is achieved due to mergers. This is known as financial synergy and this type of synergy leads to merger gains.

(f) Strategic realignment to changing environments:

Strategic planning is concerned with the firm's environments and constituencies, not just operating decisions. The strategic planning approach to mergers implies either the possibilities of economies of scale or tapping underused capacity in the firm's present managerial capabilities. The speed of adjustment to the change in the environment through the merger would be quicker than internal development. Developing the required skills and managerial capabilities internally would be time-consuming and difficult. Mergers provide an easy route to overcome these.

(g) Undervaluation:

If a certain firm is undervalued, it is quite likely that another firm would want to acquire it.

Reasons for undervaluation:

i. Underutilization of assets by management.
ii. Difference between the market value of assets and replacement cost.
iii. Acquirers have inside information.

2. Information and Signalling

(a) Information theory:

It has been observed frequently that the value of shares of the target firm increases even if the tender offer goes unsuccessful.

The reasons:

- The tender offer disseminates information that the target shares are undervalued. It is also known as **sitting on the goldmine.**
- The offer compels the target firm to perform well on its own.
- Another view is that people expect that the company will be taken over by someone else.

(b) Signaling theory:

Certain actions of the firm give signals to the market due to which the firm benefits. For example, investors use the face amount of debt that the manager decides to issue as a signal of the firm's probable performance. If the optimum amount of debt to be held by a company is D. Say there are 2 types of firms A and B. A will be successful, and B will be unsuccessful. If the firm issues debt more than D, then is termed type A, if less than D, then type B. Firm B should signal its unsuccessfulness only if the benefit from telling the truth is greater than that produced by telling lies.

Signaling may be involved in mergers in a number of ways. The fact that a firm has received a tender offer may signal to the market that hitherto unrecognized extra values are possessed by the firm or that future cash flow streams are likely to rise. When a bidder firm uses common stock in buying another firm, this may be taken as a signal by the target and others that the common stock of the bidder firm is overvalued. When business firms repurchase their shares, the market may take this as a signal that management has information that its shares are undervalued and that favourable new growth opportunities will be achieved.

3. Agency Problems and Managerialism:

(a) Agency Problems:

An agency problem arises when managers own only a small portion of the ownership shares of the firm. This partial ownership may cause managers to work less vigorously than otherwise and to consume more perquisites because the majority owners bear most of the cost. Agency problems arise because:

Contracts between managers (decision or control agents) and owners cannot be costlessly written and enforced.

Agency costs include:

    i. Cost of structuring contracts.
    ii. Costs of monitoring and controlling the behaviour of agents.
    iii. Costs of taking guarantee that agents will make the optimal decision.
    iv. Residual loss to principals (majority shareholders).
    v. Takeovers are a solution to agency problems.

(b) Managerialism:

This theory argues that the agency problem is not solved and the merger activity is a manifestation of the agency problems of inefficient external investments by managers.

4. Hubris Hypothesis:

Managers commit errors of over-optimism in evaluating merger opportunities due to excessive pride, animal spirits, or Hubris. So the whole merger movement is based on taking the hubris hypothesis as the null hypothesis and disproving it.

5. Free Cash Flow Hypothesis:

Major conflicts between managers and shareholders arise over the payment of free cash flows. Free cash flows are basically profits after all the expenses are deducted. The distribution of these profits becomes the main point of contention. Agency costs result from these conflicts of interest that can never be resolved perfectly. Takeovers can help reduce these costs.

6. Market Power:

The concentration of power with a few firms through merger activities and collusions leads to better gains.

7. Tax Benefits:

Mergers can help in reducing the tax effect. If one firm is a loss-making one, then the losses of this firm can be carried over to the profits of the other firm. This will reduce the overall profit and hence reduce the tax. Assets would be valued on a stepped up basis and hence there would be an added depreciation benefit. Ordinary gains can be substituted for capital gains and tax liabilities can be reduced.

Bibliography

Andre, P., Kooli, M., & L'Her, J.-F. (2004). The long run performance of mergers and acquisitions: Evidence from the Canadian Stock Market. *Financial Management, 33*(4), 27-43.

Capron, L. (1999). The long term performance of horizontal acquisitions. *Strategic Management Journal, 20*(11), 987-1018.

Capron, L., & Pistre, N. (2002). When do acquirers earn abnormal returns? *Strategic Management Journal, 23*(9), 781-794.

Carow, K., Heron, R., & Saxton, T. (2004). Do early bird get the returns? An empirical investigation of early mover advantages in acquisitions. *Strategic Management Journal, 25.*

Datta, D. K., Pinches, G. E., & Narayanan, V. K. (1992). Factors Influencing Wealth Creation from Mergers and Acquisitions: A Meta-Analysis. *Strategic Management Journal, 13*(1), 67-84.

DeLong, G. (2003). Do long term performance of mergers match market expectations? *Financial Managment, 32*(2), 5-25.

Elgers, P. T., & Clark, J. J. (1980). Merger Types and Shareholder Returns: Additional Evidence. *Financial Management, 9*(2), 66-72.

Freund, S., Prezas, A. P., & Vasudevan, G. K. (2003). Operating Performance and free cash flow of Asset Buyers. *Financial Management, 32*(4), 87-106.

Jarrell, G. A., & Poulsen, A. (1989). The Returns to acquiring firms in tender offers: The evidence from three decades. *Financial Management, 18*(3), 12-19.

Kummer, C. (2008). The success of Mergers and Acquisitions depends on people. *HRM Review,* 11-13.

Loderer, C., & Martin, K. (1990). Coporate Acquisitions of Listed Firms: The experience of a comprehensive sample. *Financial Management, 19*(4), 17-33.

Lubatkin, M. (1987). Merger Strategies and Stockholder Value. *Strategic Management Journal, 8*(1), 39-53.

Neely, W. P. (1987). Banking Acquisitions: Acquirer and Target Shareholder Returns. *Financial Management, 16*(4), 66-74.

Opler, T. C. (1992). Operating Performance in Leveraged Buyouts: Evidence from 1985-1989. *Financial Management, 21*(1), 27-34.

Pettway, R. H., & Yamada, T. (1986). Mergers in Japan and their impact on Stockholders' wealth. *Financial Management, 15*(4), 43-52.

Rajan, R. G., & Prasad, E. S. (2008). Next Generation Financial Reforms for India. *Finance And Development,* 23-27.

Ramakrishnan, K. (2008). Long Term Post Merger Performance of Firms in India. *Vikalpa, 33*(2), 47-63.

Ramaswamy, K., & Waegelein, J. P. (2003). Firm Financial Performance Following Mergers. *Review of Quantitative Finance and Accounting, 20*(2), 115-126.

Shick, R. A., & Jen, F. C. (1974). Merger Benefits to shareholders of acquiring firms. *Financial Management, 3*(4), 45-53.

Siegel, D. S., & Simmons, K. L. (2010). Assessing the effects of Mergers & Acquisitions on firm performance, plant productivity and workers: New Evidence from matched Employee- Employer data. *Strategic Management Journal.*

Veri, P., Lubatkin, M., Calori, R., & Viegga, J. (1997). RELATIVE STANDING AND THE PERFORMANCE OF RECENTLY ACQUIRED EUROPEAN FIRMS. *Strategic Management Journal, 18*(8).

Walker, M. M. (2000). Corporate Takeovers, Strategic Objectives, and Acquiring-Firm Shareholder Wealth. *Financial Management, 29*(1), 53-66.